Stop Hiding, You Are Valuable: Explore Your Dreams, Master Your Vision, Dominate Your Brilliance™ and by Golly, Strut Your Amazing Life.

Wake Up Girl,
YOU ARE WORTHY!
GLOBAL EDITION

FUMI HANCOCK
BESTSELLING AUTHOR

Psychiatric Mental Health Doctor of Nurse Practice, TEDx Int'l. Speaker, *Your Global Vision Midwife™ & LifeRehab™ Ambassador*

FOREWORD BY
Paula Mosher Wallace
BLOOM TODAY TV SHOW, Telly Award winning Host & TV Producer

DR. HANCOCK IS GIVING A FREE CHAPTER OF HER INSPIRATIONAL LIFE NUGGETS VIDEO SERIES - EXCLUSIVE TO HER VIP READERS GROUP:
http://bit.ly/millionaireinfluencersecrets

ISBN 978-0-9905848-8-9

Wake Up Girl,
YOU ARE WORTHY!
GLOBAL EDITION

FUMI HANCOCK
BESTSELLING AUTHOR

Psychiatric Mental Health Doctor of Nurse Practice,
TEDx Int'l. Speaker, *Your Global Vision Midwife*™ *&*
LifeRehab™ *Ambassador*

Wake Up Girl,
YOU ARE WORTHY!
Stop Hiding, You Are Valuable: Explore Your Dreams, Master Your Vision, Dominate Your Brilliance™ and by Golly, Strut Your Amazing Life.
GLOBAL EDITION

More Books in *Your Vision Torch*™ Series
Daily Vision Nuggets
Wise Quotes for Life, Home, & Business
A Success Blueprint
AVAILABLE ON AMAZON

Fumi Stephanie Hancock, DNP.
The Princess of Suburbia ® Brand
Psychiatric Mental Health Doctor of Nurse Practice
TEDx Int'l. Speaker, *Your Global Vision*™ *& LifeRehab*™ *Ambassador*

EMAIL(s):
askdrfumi@webpsychnp.com
successlaunchbp@theprincessofsuburbia.com

WEBSITE(S):
https://bit.ly/millionaireinfluencersecrets
www.drfumihancock.com / www.theprncessofsuburbia.com

MASTERCLASSES:
www.storytellerbistro.com

BLOG(S):
www.yourinneryou.com

FACEBOOK(S):
https://www.facebook.com/DrPrincessFumiHancockNP/

WATCH & SUBSCRIBE TO MY POPULAR TV SHOW
https://www.facebook.com/IAmPrincessofSuburbiaTV/
https://www.youtube.com/c/princessofsuburbia

DR. HANCOCK IS GIVING FREE INSPIRATIONAL VIDEO SERIES, ***LIFEREHAB™ NUGGETS***. THIS IS EXCLUSIVE TO HER VIP READERS GROUP:
http://bit.ly/millionaireinfluencersecrets

DO YOU WANT FREE INSPIRATIONAL LifeRehab™ VIDEO NUGGETS?

I am **ready to position** myself as an expert in my industry. I thought of writing a book or perhaps co-authoring with a bestselling author but I don't know how to start. **Can You Help Me?**

SUCESS BEGINS WITH INSPIRATION
Get your FREE 6-part inspirational video series!

"I Am An Advanced Nurse Practitioner.
Books & Documentaries Are My Legs to the World."
-Dr. Fumi Hancock

CREATE YOUR OWN OPPORTUNITIES. FIND OUT!
Receive my video series, empowering podcasts, practical tips & tools, inspiring "vision rehab" delivered directly to your inbox!

http://bit.ly/millionaireinfluencersecrets

A Paradigm Shift

FROM SAUDI ARABIA - DR. PRINCESS FUMI HANCOCK

Your Brilliance is Your Millions ™

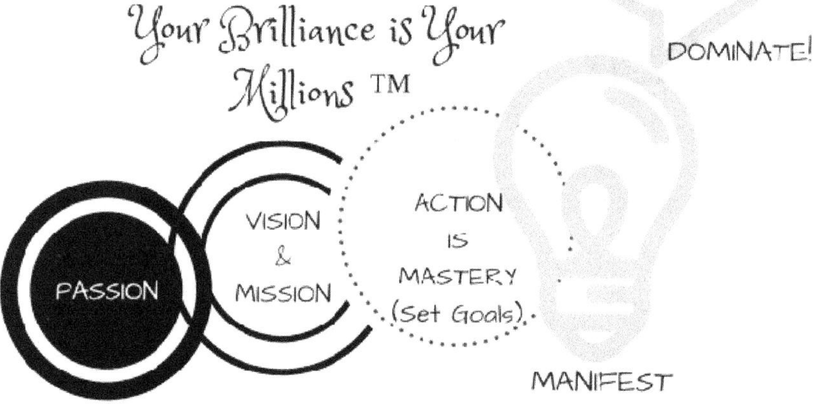

DEDICATION

To my wonderful husband, Dr. David Allen Hancock, there are no words to tell you how blessed I am that GOD thought it fit to give us both another chance at love. Thank you for loving me despite all the "ups and downs." Many may have thought we would not make it but daily, you show me love knows no boundaries neither does it see color. It is such a blessing to be your wife.

To my terrific children, Bola Winston Thompson, Demola Morounranti Thompson, my goodness… your unconditional love and the way you have blossomed to be great God-fearing young men… I am just grateful that you took the life lessons mama taught you in our difficult times and you have grown from it all. You my dear sons have turned sorrow into dancing again for me.

To my parents, Prince Ademola & Princess Remi (Alale) Ogunleye, you continue to teach and remind us of the divine creator's unsurmountable power over our lives. I cherish getting those powerful daily messages from you. Many times, I have had to go back and just read them to get strength for the day.

In all my 20 books prior to this one, I have never taken the time to truly appreciate my family…. So, in this book, I have decided to list their names.

A huge thank you to my family, Attorney Lara & Dr. Kunle Ojebuoboh, Mide & Juwon (their children); Mojisola

Adetutu and my beautiful niece and nephews: Dami,, Zainab and Rasaaq; Adesoji Ogunleye my brother who continues to hold strong regardless of how stormy the weather is; my sweet…sweet brother, Muyiwa Thomas & Abigail Fagbemi (children: Mercy & Joel), thanks for all of your generous hearts, Dr. Olajide & Dr. Abimbola Kolawole and the 3 kings, Kolade, Dipo and Niyi, Lolade Ogunleye and her beautiful twins (Remi and Timi), I love you all.

As one who hails from a royal household, I come from a big family that ten pages will possibly not cover. So, I ask for forgiveness ahead if I do not mention your name here. It's not an oversight, I see you all and thank you for your prayers and support. Mr. Femi & Titi Adeyemi (Bunmi, Jumoke and family), Mr. Femi & Moladun Abu family, I see you too. All the Ogunleye, Odundun lineage and the Adumori Nigerian Royal Household who has ruled Emure Ekiti Kingdom since the 12100ADs, I thank you. Our royal father, King Emmanuel Adebayo, you are deeply loved and appreciated. May God grant you long life to continue leading our communities according to God's standards. Aunty Tope Akinkuotu, you are a great support.

Recently, I reconnected with a true leader of leaders… a brother who continues to pick my calls whenever I needed a sounding board, Former Governor of Ekiti State and Current Party Chairman, Chief Olusegun Oni. Many have given up on Nigerian politics… many believe there is no hope for Nigeria. I believe we are not asking for perfection as there is no one perfect but God's grace covers it all. I truly appreciate you. You have made yourself easy access to this little fifty-something year old gal with a dream. I dream one day when our giant, Nigeria, will arise out of constant chaos and crisis and will take her place rightfully so.

A big thank you to Apostle Solomon Buckley of Fresh wind International for seeing in me what dome didn't. A special shout-out to World Changers Sister-Tribe™ who are now part of my Prayer-Preneur™ Network, for making my life so full. Sisters and brothers, you know who you are. Continuous thanks to my Doctor of Nurse Practice Cohort who are rocking their prospective area(s) of influence. Dr. Ruth Felton, Dr Monica Leverette, Dr. Leonora Muhammed, Dr. Willa Thompson – I thank you all for your continuous support- either purchasing my book or seeing me through my psychiatric- mental health nurse practitioner board exam. Whew! Thank you to Monica Schmelter, General manager, WHTN Christian Television, Nashville, TN and oh my, Paula Mosher Wallace, President of Bloom in the Dark, Inc. and Host of Bloom Today for connecting me with such a powerhouse classy woman who rocks her place in the media industry.

Finally, big kudos to my readers, reviewers and bloggers… I owe you a debt of gratitude.

"Dr. Princess Fumi shares the message of hope in the midst of tragedy."
~ **Star Ledger**

TABLE OF CONTENTS

DEDICATION.. IX
FOREWORD XVII
A LOVE LETTER FROM YOUR GLOBAL VISION
    MIDWIFE™ & LIFEREHAB ™ AMBASSADOR
   XXV
PREAMBLE... 1
PREFACE 5
INTRODUCTION 23
1. DISCOVER OR REDISCOVER YOUR PASSION 45
2. IGNITE YOUR PASSION.................................. 73
3. LAUNCH YOUR PASSION 87
4. LIVE OUT YOUR PASSION 101
5. TURN YOUR PASSION INTO PROFIT.............113
6. GROW YOUR PASSION 129
7. SUSTAIN YOUR PASSION 139
8. PAY IT FORWARD 147
CONCLUSION.. 155
ABOUT THE AUTHOR.. 203
MORE RESOURCES 207

Enjoyed this book? Want to leave a **Review**?
successlaunchbp@theprincessofsuburbia.com

FOREWORD

PAULA MOSHER WALLACE
Bloom Today TV Show, Host & Producer
President, Bloom in the Dark, Inc.

You Are Worthy!

"But I'm not perfect...."

I'm walking through the woods on a beautiful summer evening, wondering why God didn't make me perfect. At eighteen, I feel like I should be put together. I'm an adult now, right? Shouldn't I know who I am by now? But I'm not happy with who I am. Everywhere I look, I see beauty. God made these beautiful trees, fluffy clouds, yellow flowers. They are so amazing!

Then, I picture myself looking in the mirror this afternoon before my walk. I see myself as awkward, too skinny, braces. My long blonde curls are pretty, and I like the color of my eyes but the rest of me is all wrong.....

God, why didn't you just make me perfect?

I'm thinking that perfect means that I look like the Venezuelan Miss Universe with a warm complexion, high cheekbones, long wavy dark hair, big eyes, and the perfect figure. Perfect means no self-doubt, absolute confidence, a permanent smile.... It means that my boyfriend would never have broken up with me. He would have wanted to marry me. Perfect--is what I'm not.

Then it hit me. I was talking to my Creator! In fact, I talk to Him all the time. Some people call that prayer or meditation. I call it a running dialog.

If you were perfect, you wouldn't need ME God whispered in my soul. Of course, I would still need Him. But if I was perfect, why would I need Him? Lucifer lost everything when he thought he no longer needed his creator. Would I really lose that dependence on Him if I didn't have my problems? I count on Him for everything. My heart and soul look to Him for meaning and help, constantly.

In your weakness, I am made strong suddenly took on an entirely different meaning for me. I don't need to be perfect to be the perfect vessel for Him to use for great things. Maybe I'm not perfect by my standards, but just maybe, God made me perfect for His plan for my life. He made me "worthy" in Him.

As I was asking God about how He's made us worthy, this scene from my life came back to me. It reminded me of a lesson He's taken me back to repeatedly. My worthiness is ONLY found in my relationship with God. Not because I run a ministry that is touching hearts globally. Not because I have a television show in 204 countries on 15 networks in 4 languages. Not because I won a Telly Award. Not because I'm an author, speaker, TV show host, producer, podcaster, life coach, curriculum creator, ministry leader, nonprofit president, entrepreneur, manager.... I'm intrinsically worthy IN Christ. Period.

I'm so grateful for Pastor Doctor Princess Fumi Hancock being a living example of how God makes us "worthy" in Him.

When I first met her, I was absolutely blown away by meeting a real princess! Over the last several years, I have been even more blown away by getting to know the person underneath all the titles.

I'm amazed by the incredible blessings of birthright, training, and accomplishments that Princess carries. They absolutely fit the amazing person God created baby Fumi to be.

Baby Fumi was worthy without any of those titles. Because God created her as His special daughter. She was worthy despite all the damage others did to her. She was worthy despite the devastation she experienced. She was worthy as she bore children that God designed her to be the mother for. She was worthy as she fought for her life and the lives of her children. She was worthy as she learned everything she could to help others. She was worthy as she ran to God repeatedly for her identity to be found in Him!

Reverend Doctor Princess Fumi Hancock is worthy because she's walking in her calling despite everything that has tried to stop her. She's worthy because she's made in the image of the Highest God.

Each one of us is worthy because God is worthy, and we are His children.

PAULA MOSHER WALLACE
Bloom Today TV, Telly Award winning Host & TV Producer
President, Bloom in the Dark, Inc.

YOLANDA DUPREE
Bestselling Author & President
Dupree Empowerment Group Inc.

When I reflect over my life, there have only been few women that have richly blessed me and Dr. Fumi Hancock is one of them.

I appreciate her boldness and commitment to not only her success but to the success of other women as well.

Although I've only known Dr. Hancock for 2 years, she has truly inspired me because she is a woman of her word and I trust her relationship with God.

All Praise to God for connecting me with such a great woman!

YOLANDA DUPREE
Bestselling Author & President
Dupree Empowerment Group Inc.

MARKITA D. COLLINS
Bestselling Author, Minister, Speaker, Certified Life Coach & President, Kita's Kompany

God used this woman at a pivotal time in my life where I was stuck in clay. Dr. Princess Fumi Hancock is incredible and an amazing gift. She is anointed, called and equipped to help birth out Visionaries' with ideas, book concepts and/or movies. You name it, she got it.

Dr. Princess Fumi Hancock's relationship with me was purely organic. It was not contrived nor by coincidence. Our connection was not tainted by noises but simply pure and genuine love. Dr. Princess Fumi's love for not just God but to see people succeed and to walk in their purpose fuels her beyond money and titles.

I have seen her work tirelessly to see everyone around her come up while she puts her needs to the side. I pray that one day she really gets the honor that she deserves but I'll start with me by simply saying thank you Dr. Princess Fumi for not allowing me to miscarry, for not allowing me to abort what was already inside of me I love and appreciate you. You are truly one of God 's chosen.

MARKITA D. COLLINS
Bestselling Author, Minister, Speaker,
Certified Life Coach & President, Kita's Kompany

A Love Letter from Your Global Vision Midwife™ & LifeRehab ™ Ambassador

~Dr. Fumi Stephanie Hancock, DNP.

Allow me to clear the Air!

Listen up! College Students, Newly College Graduates, Speakers, Coaches/ Trainers, Creatives, "Career-Professionals, Corporate Climbers, Government Leaders, Intrapreneurs, Entrepreneurs, Prayerpreneurs and all the -Preneurs in the world, this system will touch you.

For those who are familiar with my writing, you know this by now! None of my books are simply books! They are often not a standalone read! They are systems designed to help you reach your destination. They are interconnected and often, if picked up and read, will take you to a place where you truly are not only exploring but mastering who you are and what you are supposed to be doing.

Having said that, here I go again, just as I stated in YOUR VISION TORCH Series… this too is not a book but an innovative program! As with all my books, they are geared to help you move from *where you are* to *where you ought to be.* Therefore, as an innovative system, it will require a lot of you. It will insist that you be a participant in your own success journey. It will push you to think, address, and confront issues you would ordinarily sweep under the rug.

Wake Up Girl, YOU ARE WORTHY! So, Strut Your Amazing Life will require you to tell the truth, tear the veil™, and unmask the hidden parts of you that have literally set you back for years! This is a Life & Vision Rehab™ process and you my friend are the mission. However, this will not indulge you in pity parties, but it will empower you with practical tools to help you not only discern your purpose, or perhaps ignite it, it will equally provide you thought-provoking life mastery skills that EVERYONE needs to unleash their inner rock star!

With this system, you are going to go deeper, if you so choose, and YOU WILL GET RESULTS! You don't know how much it meant to me when my husband read it and told me how much he enjoyed reading this book. That type of compliment does not come cheap and easy from my husband who is a scholar and therefore looks at many reads from that perspective.

Now, if you are ready to begin the work, welcome and get ready for a life changing experience. As I always say at all my events:

This is an Epic Event, a Kairos Moment!

One Event Elects Who You Are;

One Event Molds Your Values & Beliefs;

One Event Charts the Course of Your Journey…
Good or Bad;

One Event Determines Your Destiny;

And One Event Will Change Your Life Forever!

Please note that as we proceed on this journey, I will continue to use the following words interchangeably: Entrepreneur and Professional Intrapreneur. Afterall, if you are still working at a company, that is part of your life and you are a professional intrapreneur.

THE TOOLS HERE CHANGED MY LIFE FOREVER AND THEY CONTINUE TO DO SO DAILY. THEY CAN AND WILL CHANGE YOURS TOO IF YOU SIMPLY STAY OPEN.

DR. DAVID ALLEN HANCOCK, DM.
Loving Husband

"Happy is the man who finds a true friend, and far happier is he who finds that true friend in his wife." Franz Schubert

I want to say a bit about my wife, Princess Fumi... never have I known a woman of such dedication and strength... to quote Shakespeare, to endure the slings and arrows of outrageous fortune. Yet she perseveres, always stretching herself to the next goal... for those familiar with the Bible, she is, to me, a prime example of a Proverbs 31 woman and is a blessing to me, her husband. She's there for me when I need her and there for others, often exceeding her energy to do so. She's a friend, a guide, a partner... a true Christian woman in every sense... and so I rarely compare myself to her, but simply watch in amazement as she goes!

DR. DAVID ALLEN HANCOCK, DM.
(Loving Husband)

We are all uniquely designed, for a unique purpose, to uniquely impact our world.
DR. PRINCESS FUMI HANCOCK

"Upanishad"

...Now, sit at the feet of the master....

PREAMBLE

No Apologies Here!

If what you have been doing is not working, it is time to fearlessly partner in your own success rescue and recovery™.

One Event Can Change Your Life Forever! Make this journey an event that will open you up to new possibilities!

Each year, many people look for ways to ensure that their vision, dreams, and life purpose are fulfilled. Sadly, each year goes by and goals intended to be fulfilled go untouched. We get sidetracked by the same life we are trying to make sense of.

This book, *Wake Up Girl,* YOU ARE WORTHY. *So, Strut Your Amazing Life,* while it sits comfortably in a non-judgment zone, the concepts and precepts will be in your face as with many of my books! Some ideas are revealed in a subtle manner while others may be straight up hard to swallow. We all know that the truth about who we are is often hard to swallow. I know!

Here is my warning, you will most times feel a tingle in the pit of your stomach when you are faced with some truths about who you are and what role you have played in ensuring your current placement in life. As a Psychiatric Mental Health Nurse Practitioner, I love one of Yalom's Theory of

Existentialism. Well, it appears to be mouth full when saying it out loud, but here are some propositions he made. I am obviously paraphrasing:

He stated that because we exist, we experience an infinity of emotions that often lead to endless life searching questions. Therefore, we are constantly searching for answers… mostly to our "why". Yalom, in his nursing theory, provided 5 decisive concerns of humanity. He explained further:

1. That human beings exist without any apparent cause or reason.

2. That human beings have freedom and with that freedom comes responsibilities.

3. That human beings, no matter how much we love one another, at some point will have to walk the journey called life alone.

4. That death is inevitable, so we must get over it and make our lives count for something.

5. Without you taking charge and owning your life, it is meaningless (source: goodtherapy.org).

Here is the truth about this *wake-up* journey, if you dare to walk through the painful process, you will eventually get to the power packed awesome happy realization that will encourage you to begin taking massive actions.

Regardless of what time of the year you are picking this game changing system up, you will be equipped to manifest wonderful breakthroughs in your life, starting with your thought process, as failure often begins with thoughts before it physically manifests. However, realize that it will take persistence, relentless effort, intentional massive actions, patience, God's favor, patience… did I say God's favor and patience? And yes, the appointed time to birth your purpose in its fullness.

Life will always dish us the good, the bad, the ugly.
What we do and how we respond is what ultimately
determines our outcome.
It's time to take your temperature for how you are doing.
DR. PRINCESS FUMI HANCOCK

PREFACE
The Easy Road to Unfulfilled Goals!

You must continually declare positive words upon your life, the lives of your loved ones and your ventures.

If you are frustrated about unfulfilled goals; if you are overwhelmed and feel a sense of being stuck in one place; if you are looking for ways to catapult from where you are now, if you are somewhat discontented and dissatisfied with life; if you are ready to leap from where you are to where you ought to be (i.e. triumphant, overcoming, fulfilled, financially free), or perhaps you are at the point of giving up, may be you are excelling in your career/business and you just need some tips to push you even higher, then hear this, YOU NEED A PROVEN & INNOVATIVE STRATEGY FOR SUCCESS!. You may be attempting to recover success or boost it. Either way, welcome to THE EXPERIENCE. Finally, if you feel unappreciated and overworked, yet love what you do and are looking for ways to monetize it, you are in the right place too.

The road to lack of progress, perpetual lack of self-worth, failure and persistent demotion is easy and wide. Sadly, it is a path tread by many and no matter how much we declare and decree empowering words daily, if concrete and intentional steps are not taken to avoid certain pit falls in our lives, we will join the people who daily find themselves in the dump… the sea of failure, that is.

> *We teach people*
> *how to treat us.*

In my book, YOUR VISION TORCH series, I shared a 2013 Gallup Poll that reported that 70% of Americans hate their jobs. According to Forbes, 70% of employees hate their jobs, meaning that unhappy employees outnumber the happy by more than two to one. Deloitte's Shift Index in 2013 reported that 80% are dissatisfied with their jobs. Business Insider in 2010 posed this question: though 80% hate their jobs, they asked… should you choose a passion or a paycheck? Interestingly, a 2013 CNBC report proved it… that many would choose following their true passion or job satisfaction over office perks! People are simply getting more and more dissatisfied, disengaged, disconnected, and overwhelmed by the demands of their current career path. They feel something is missing and they are not fulfilled. Lack of self-worth is on the rise as people are constantly experiencing being back-stabbed by those they care about. With low self-worth comes low self-esteem. As one's self-esteem diminishes, fear sets in and failure takes its permanent abode on ones' home.

For those who say they have found themselves on a path to their calling, good for you. Registered Nurses who would most often claim this report that they are overworked, stressed out, feel unheard, overwhelmed, underappreciated, and at times devalued.

For years, after the afore-mentioned reports, things have not improved. In fact, it has worsened. People are being mistreated at their places of work or other relationships. Many are forced to work like machines. Many employees' spirits are broken beyond repair! Yet management is not sensitive to the silent cries of their employees.

I remember sharing my concerns with one "Manager" and he said to me, the same people that you think will break and finally quit will not. I asked him why not? His response was we are the top paying company in the area, so they will not quit. My question then was, does that give you the right to break peoples' spirits?

Why am I sharing this? I share this to say that *we teach people how to treat us*! Many of us have become another person's door mat because WE CHOSE IT! Even as a door mat, there is a payoff for us. I know this may be hard to comprehend but think of it for a second. Why would any rational minded person allow another to dump on them?

Truth be told, many of us do not see ourselves as overcomers. We tell people what seems right at that moment, but we do not truly see ourselves achieving more than we are at that very moment.

You are hardworking, you know your stuff, you have mastered your brilliance and brilliantly if I may add; you are a genius in your own right… you may not understand how things work in one field, you have certainly mastered your sphere of genius. Yet you will allow people to abuse you, abuse your brilliance, and then turn around to promote someone else who just landed a few hours ago… landed right on top of you! Why would you be okay with this, if there is no payoff for you?

Are you living out your vision daily? Are you living it out loud and are you living your life the way it is meant to be? Or are you merely surviving? Do you understand that you are worthy of all the greatness the creator has orchestrated for you?

You didn't find your calling, but your calling found you.

Hear this… you deserve to live a full life, one that feeds you emotionally, physically, and spiritually. Regardless of your previous life experiences or what you might have gone through last night, or even one second ago, you were born to succeed and created for excellence! Stop hiding behind others… quit hiding behind what you perceive as your inadequacies. Come out and live life loud!

It is amazing what you will accept when you are in your twenties but will not accept in 40s' or even 50s' but then again, there are people who have not developed well! Understanding who you are, what you were created for, will show you your "why forward".

On this journey, I will consistently ask you this simple question: How have you been living out your vision or passion? It is certainly my goal that, as you read this book, you will consider the masterclass at: www.storytellerbistro.com called *7 Days to Release Your Amazing Life*. While this book gives you a look at how to be successful, the masterclass is in-depth videos and will provide opportunities for practice.

As I write this book, I sit in my apartment in Saudi Arabia! That's right! For years, I have been known as a Global Vision Midwife™ across all my social media platforms and internationally. It was only prudent that, at some point in my life, I would not be flying in and out of countries, rather settle down to understand a culture.

We all have different seasons in our lives. There is a season to be still while being tutored or mentored, that is, to be the mentee. To avoid the easy road to unfulfilled goals, you must learn to discern the season you are in. Because your best friend is in a season of speaking globally does not mean you are. Because everyone around you is writing books does not mean you were called to write one. Because everyone is turning to entrepreneurship, does not mean you need to turn your life upside down to become an overnight entrepreneur. You just might be a professional intrapreneur.

> *When we get desperate, we begin to steal from others, particularly those who have entrusted us with their discoveries.*

I can't tell you how many people show up on my social media platform, my broadcast or blog asking for help on how to "find their passion." In fact, I have had senior executives and ministers turn to me asking for help! They are successful at what they do as managers, some make loads of money doing what they do, but they feel a gap in the pit of their stomachs. They understand that there are things that operate for and against them which are often beyond what they can see. They know they need to start planning as they know that whatever gravy train they are on right now would not last! More importantly, they are afraid to make any moves because of the fear of losing the income they are accustomed to. Isn't it therefore amazing to see that both the wealthy and the poor share the same fears and uncertainties? The only difference is that one does it in style with money in the pocket while the other struggles through life.

I challenge you to pick up your torch, fight for your life, and make an intentional decision to live an amazing life!

Fight for what is rightfully yours and just don't sit back expecting God or someone to hand over what was stolen from you. For those of us who read the Bible, Jeremiah 4: 14 – 15 impacted in me complete healing and boldness to go after what is mine! In these verses, the awesomeness of God was displayed. More importantly, his children were instructed never to be afraid of their enemies. The sweetest and most revealing part for me was verse 15, which clearly states that the plans of our enemies (frenemies) God has exposed. More importantly, your enemies have found out that God reveals their wicked exploits to you. In addition, they have now known that the heavy anointing of frustration they are experiencing is not directly from the one they thought they wanted to attack. Rather, the coals of fire are coming from God the Father, God the Son, and God the Holy Spirit.

In Your Vision Torch™ series, I share some stories. As a master storyteller, I believe that you can learn from other persons' stories. And so, I continue here… worthy of greatness

A Life Lesson from "The Hurricane," a blockbuster movie on America.

A short while ago, I watched a movie called "the Hurricane" (1999) and in it, a black man who was uprising in the field of boxing was railroaded. Never mind that he was also naïve, ignorant, and somewhat pompous when he was growing up. From the movie, it seemed like when he was rising in that field, he didn't think anything, or anyone could touch him! He was wrong! For over twenty years of his young adult life, he lived in a penitentiary for a crime he did not commit! He was subdued. His spirit was broken, and his pride shattered… he watched those who were behind him disappear one at the time and was left alone in the penitentiary to face his situation. Stay with me, I am going somewhere with this story. At first, he fought hard for his release and every time his hopes of going back to his family became grim. At some point, he stated that he finally gave up and turned to his "reality", that he would live the rest of his life in the penitentiary. Denzel Washington played the lead role and, oh my, as usual, he was spectacular! The actual star and Hurricane himself, is Rubin Carter! In this movie, there were two statements he made that just incredibly moved me:

"Hate put me in prison and now, love is going to bust me out!"
— Rubin Carter

The second statement was even more profound than the first. He started off by sharing his innermost thoughts about writing with a character of interest, Vicellous Shannon's character, "Lesra". According to Hurricane, writing was a powerful tool… one he used to get his mind right. Writing was his sanity instrument… one that impacted not only him, but those around him and the global community. Rubin Carter, in the movie, was impacting the global community from behind the prison! He had resolved to himself that he might never get out of the prison, but his life would make a difference in the global community! He may have given up on the fight to come out of prison, but he had resigned that his "strokes of pen" would change peoples' mindset… what he didn't have growing up! Little did he know that the same stroke of pen was going to "burst" him out of prison for good.

Where am I going with this powerful story?
Never give up on fighting for your life, no matter how grim things may look today! Secondly, what you put out, you will get back! So be careful what you are putting out. If you choose to be reckless with your life, reckless results will find you! Sadly, that same reckless decision may cost you your life, home, family, career, and business. We all have made bad decisions and half of us today, including myself, are sitting right in the middle of the outcome of these unfortunate decisions. Many have died in the middle of their outcomes and never resolved anything; some have literally taken their own lives because they couldn't live with their decisions and outcomes. If you are reading this, I am glad you are alive to do it over the right way! Ruben Carter got another lease in life through the strokes of his pen. He did not stew in his misery but channeled it into impacting the lives of others with his writing.

The Hurricane story has impacted me deeply and even given me increased dedication and greater insight into my writing career. That it is not what I can take for granted! This movie has truly affected me in such a way that I have a better understanding of the role I play in society. That through my writing, I can change a life! He said, "I transcend the place that holds me through writing" What a powerful revelation.

So today, in this book, *Wake Up Girl*, YOU ARE WORTHY. By golly Strut Your Amazing Life, I charge you as Your Global Vision Midwife™, to transcend the places that have held you bound. Whatever may have caused you to give up on certain dreams… whatever may have demanded that you no longer pay attention to your passion… whatever may have convinced you that you are not meant to live your best life, whatever whispers you hear about your lack of self-worth, I want you to put it aside today. I want you to pay close attention to your surroundings. I need for you to go back and dig deep down inside of your battered and shattered soul; I need for you to intentionally declare that BREAKTHROUGH HAS COME and what has held you bound before will no longer have a hold on you. It doesn't matter if you don't even know how to climb out of the bondage yet or that challenge. You begin at a place where your soul has finally found rest. Channel that "rest" into a gifting and allow your brilliance to shine enough to change a life. This is what this book is about. Today, I step up to allow my brilliance to shine regardless of whoever may choose to pick up this book to read.

Just as I often do in other books and broadcasts, I tear down the veil and allow my brilliance to touch a life. If you are engaged in this book, then you are that soul I have been called to impact.

Another lesson gotten from the Hurricane movie. Things did not start moving in his favor until he became passionate and convinced that it was time for him to get out of the prison! His passion and intense drive, understanding what he stood to lose… which was that his case was never ever going to be heard ever again in any courts if his newly found evidence was thrown out of the Supreme Court. Whatever we may be going through, we must be intensely passionate about finding a solution. Just as a boxer gets knocked down and he gets back up again into the ring to finish the fight, we too must stand for our vision, our purpose, our passion in life! I know you may have been hurt by many in and out of church, nevertheless, you must arise like the eagle you are. Shake o ff the low self-esteem or perhaps anger… let the real hero in you arise. Just because you know what you are called to doesn't mean it will

automatically happen! Wake Up Girl! Shake the pain loose…
turn your pain into fuel and walk in victory.

> *The bigger the dream, the bigger your adversary… the bigger the hurdle to fulfill that dream.*

For every big dream you know you are meant to fulfill, or whatever dream you are yet to discover, there are persons, places, things ready in the wings to distract you from getting to your destination.

Do not be your own nightmare!

Ruben Carter underestimated what "people" could do and he left himself vulnerable. He felt making it in the boxing arena meant he had clout enough to get himself out of the pickle he found himself in. Little did he know! We must never underestimate the kinds of trouble people, places, and things can get us into, when we leave ourselves vulnerable to them. Often, when I talk about "persons", the first thing on our minds are "people" other than ourselves… you begin to think about the last friendship you had that went sour, the relationship where you were dumped, treated badly, or the close family member who behaved badly to us. While this may be so, the greatest enemy you have is YOU. You can be your worst nightmare or your greatest cheer leader. It is all in perspective. When you loathe yourself, talk yourself down, underestimate your own gifting, allow people to chew you up and spit you out… when you are so quick to judge yourself, when you fail to listen and take directions, you are dragging yourself down the pipeline of failure. If you are out there feeling devalued or you devalue yourself, know that YOU are your nightmare! It is easy to get rid of a toxic relationship, remove yourself from a JOB that is working you too hard and unreasonably. However, what is more difficult to do is getting rid of your own toxic self. We cannot remove ourselves from US. We live with ourselves and must face the dancing drum of our lives, whether we want to or not. Though we can't remove US, there are steps we must take to ensure that our dreams, aspirations, hopes, vision, and mission… whatever you call it… does not self-destruct!

As a writer, I am forever grateful that the Creator allowed me to write. So, I do not take the stroke of my pen lightly or my mastermind, and success club. In writing this book, I know that wisdom is oozing out and bouncing onto my tablet. So today, I urge you to remove doubt, shame, fear, feelings of unworthiness and not being more than enough, out of your vocabulary.

Expectations for this Book

While some of you may be familiar with the masterclass called *7 Days to Release Your Amazing Life,* this book does not take the place of the popular masterclass. Rather, it is meant to give you a high-level preview of what it means and what it takes to release your amazing life – home, life, business/career. To begin your transformation journey today, first join the Princess of Suburbia® community for our email "bytes" at http://bit.ly/drfumisfans. Then remember the Facebook group, http://bit.ly/princessofsuburbiacommunity , where like-minded people are coming together to learn, inform, and forge alliances. Perhaps you believe you are a prayerpreneur™, then join our prayerpreneur network on Facebook.

To live the life you want, there are 7 steps that I will attempt to lay out here for you. Success does not jump on us, but we must make intentional strides to make success happen.

> *What success looks like for me may not be what it looks like for you.*

To begin this journey, let's answer the following questions:

(1). **Define What "Success" is to YOU?** I am not talking about what it looks like for the person you admire, or your parents, but what does success mean and/or look like for YOU?

This question requires a heavy dose of soul searching. Ever so often, we look around to find someone we can emulate. There is nothing wrong with this except today, the limelight is on you my friend.

Let me help you out here, as of now I am on a global journey where consulting in the Middle East is part of success for me. Therefore, success means accomplishing the goals I have set for myself and my company this year. It means using my brilliance to impact that part of the world. Today, by God's grace, I can totally say that I have been moving towards what he has called me to. It is, many times, challenging but I truly believe that I am making an impact. Amidst this journey, I ended up becoming the first African American to grace the TEDx Talk Al Anjal National Schools (https://youtu.be/IjFPKUSN3NQ) platform in Saudi Arabia. What an incredible experience that was.

Life/Home: Having strong family bonds; terrific relationship with my husband, children and extended family.

Relationship: Business- Forging strong and meaningful alliances with powerhouse entrepreneurs.

Health: Weight Loss- Keeping it off, eating right and exercising right.

Ministry / Spiritual: I will continue to use my gifting to be a blessing in my local church and that at large.

Business / Career: Assess and re-assess where I am with my area(s) of brilliance. Are they being served well? Am I on course or have I derailed? This coming year is a year of complete and good old-fashioned assessment/re-evaluation of where I am with my business. Am I making headway or am I dropping balls all over the place?

YOUR TURN:

____

____

____

____

____

____

____

____

____

____

____

Bravo, if you pushed to candidly answer those questions. For those who are attempting to skim through it, I say, DO NOT! Though this step may appear to be insignificant or too simple, it is vital that it is not skipped.

NOW, TAKE A BREAK AND COME BACK TO YOUR ANSWERS!

Having completed the above exercise, let me quickly give you a high-level description of the moving parts to this journey… your journey to living and releasing your amazing life.

In this book, *Wake Up Girl,* YOU ARE WORTHY! By Golly, Strut YOUR AMAZING LIFE, *we will explore the following:*

- **A *Love Letter* to My Tribe**
- **PREAMBLE**
- **PREFACE**
- **INTRODUCTION:** Demystifying Discovery
- **PHASE 1:** How to Discover or Rediscover Your Passion
- **PHASE 2:** How to Ignite Your Passion
- **PHASE 3:** How to Launch Your Passion and Live it
- **PHASE 4:** Live Out Your Passion
- **PHASE 5:** Turn that Passion into Profit
- **PHASE 6**: Sustain Your Passion
- **PHASE 7:** How to Grow Your Passion
- **PHASE 8:** Pay It Forward
- **ABOUT the Author**
- **MORE RESOURCES**

If you are ready to ditch the frustration failure has brought your way and you are prepared to do the work, I am ready to show you and provide to YOU with practical tools you must absolutely consider succeeding. It is time to reconcile YOU to YOUR TRUTH.

You are as great as the discovery you made about yourself &
the truth you unveil about YOU.
~DR. PRINCESS FUMI HANCOCK

INTRODUCTION
Demystifying the Process & Debunking Myths

Only you get to write your story. Only you get to define your success. Only you can make your dreams happen! ONLY YOU.

Discovering or re-discovering your passion is never easy. Sadly, we live in a world full of cynicism. The one who is supposed to love you unconditionally turns out to be your worst nightmare. Those you slaved for turn out to betray you. The same person you opened to, turns out to be the mistake of your life. You have lived in perpetual anger. You are in pain, you are disappointed in people and sometimes in yourself. You are in pain because against better judgement and against people's advice, you allowed people to get close enough to inflict pain! Nothing seems to be adding up for you. So, you have become desperate… desperate about fulfilling your destiny. You are certain if no help came, you would be in an ugly ride of your life.

If this is anywhere close to what you are experiencing, I want you to know that there is light at the end of the tunnel for you. The tunnel might not look like what you normally settle for, however, it is divinely created for you. It fits you like a glove because it was created with you on the creator's mind.

Discovering lends its ear to understanding that there are people out there who have truly not identified their passion. Some believe they know what it is, but they are having a hard time stirring it up for maximum economic impact.

> *Success begins with us fully engaged in our passion, true calling, or vision.*

To be totally engaged, you must understand the fullness of your passion. You will only get better at what you understand, practice and value. Discovery involves recovery. That is, the detection of who you truly are at the core of your being. To quickly tap into this powerful source, you must look at the whole journey as a discovery otherwise, it can be overwhelming and frustrating about your attempt to figure out what you are supposed to be doing and in what season.

Many live out their lives never fulfilling what they were called to be. The popular adage that the graveyard is filled with many books unwritten, powerful stories untold, films never directed, medical discoveries never realized, and the list goes on, is a reality and not just a cliché. Our role on the face of this earth is to live life full and leave it empty!

What you have inside of you is meant to impact the global community. Not only that, it will change the course of your life, and that of *others* around you.

To discover or rediscover your passion, there are certain candid questions you must ask yourself. Here you are essentially called to fearlessly co-partner in your own success rescue. For many of us, our passion has been hijacked by life's nuances. In which case, here you will get the tools and the know-how to recapture your success.

Let's start this journey by **debunking some myths** about discovering or rediscovering our passion. A worthy person understands that he or she must know how to discover his/her passion. If you lack self-worth, you lack the agility to not only pursue your passion but run and overtake it.

> *Housecleaning will often mean you being ready to clean out the toxic habits, things, and/or toxic people in your life!*

The road to success often requires "housecleaning." Oxford dictionary definition of housecleaning states *the removal of unwanted or superfluous items, practices, conditions, or personnel.*

Let's consider this… how would your life look like if you could achieve success, as you desire, and live the life you've always wanted to without any hindrance? How would it feel to live an amazing life unapologetically? What would it take for you to live that life and more importantly, what are you willing to do to make it happen?

I have seen people who tell me repeatedly that they are ready to work to make things happen for themselves, but sadly, when the time comes to do the work, they are nowhere to be found. Your choice to read this book or perhaps decide to take the accompanying masterclass, *7 Days to Release Your Amazing Life,* makes you one of the top 5% who are ready to push through nonsensical excuses and are ready to change their lives.

Many are not successful because they lack complete focus. They begin to do something but before they see the success of that one thing, they move on to something else or just plain self-sabotage themselves…literally shoot themselves in the foot. Are you guilty as charged? I WAS! I must consistently work at it and this work must be intentional, with accountability to a partner.

Let's demystify and debunk some myths.

(1). The removal of unwanted or superfluous items: Many times, we carry on our backs too much baggage. This heavy baggage from our past may result from issues that were self-inflicted or that originated from others, even some things created without our participation. For us to succeed, we must look in the mirror but more importantly, take a candid look at the baggage we carry: Physically, Mentally/Emotionally and Spiritually.

Which part of your life baggage may have been self-inflicted because you refused to get out of your own way? Which evolved from issues that didn't include your participation? For this exercise to be effective, you must take a hard look in the mirror and be ready to fess up to where YOU KNOW YOU DROPPED THE BALL!

ACTIVITY – 1:

Check Out the Journal: *365 Days to Release Your Vision Torch Journal: Achieve Your Dreams, Ignite Your Passion, & Re-engineer Your Life Purpose*:
https://www.amazon.com/gp/bookseries/B017WCHMHW/

(1). Are you guilty of losing focus in the middle of a project? In other words, do you dump one project for another when frustrated? Better yet, have you ever experienced when you are right the brink of a breakthrough, then you self-destruct by making a completely unexpected or decision, one which ultimately cost you a deal? If yes, then jot this down. If not, then bravo!

(2). What impact has this lack of focus or impromptu decision played in the fulfillment of your dreams?

(3). What are the self-defeating thoughts you tell yourself about your self-worth, fulfilling your destiny or living out your passion? Do they often stop you from moving forward positively with your plans?

> *You will never address what you are*
> *not wiling to face neither will you*
> *succeed when you do not understand*
> *that failure is part of success.*

Dig deeper in this exploration by signing up for the masterclass at: www.storytellerbistro.com. Here is the deal, we must strive to get rid of circumstances holding us back and those causing the "failure to launch" syndrome that plagues our lives.

Physically: What are you holding on to tightly right now that may be unhealthy for you? An unhealthy eating habit perhaps? Could it be a toxic relationship? Are you overly sexual? Are you into self-mutilation or chronic depression? Is your past having a strong grip on your life? Cleaning the house, both physically and mentally, can be very difficult.

If whatever you are holding on to does not advance your ultimate vision, **YOU MUST DITCH IT IMMEDIATELY**! You are worthy of a life God desires for you… His ultimate best. The urge to believe that "specific" things, beliefs, or even persons belong in your life for you to succeed is simply a myth that you must eliminate. We also know that *no man is an island*. However, we must invite quality people to sit at our table not time wasters!

There is the saying that "the teacher appears when the student is ready." Having a clean canvas to do it over again is proof to the divine that you are ready to progress.

THE TRUTH BE TOLD! House cleaning is not fun! If you are like me, there have been times when you just do not feel like dealing with cleaning your house. It is crucial that we look at who we are, what we have accomplished thus far, mistakes made in the past… but more importantly, what we perceive as our payoff when we steer our lives in the wrong direction. Whether we like it or not, there is a payoff for every action or inaction we take. In life, we are driven by either pain or pleasure. Which is yours?

> *Housecleaning, heart cleaning, and/or soul searching are the very first step in your success recovery.*

Practices, Conditions or Personnel: These are other words that define housecleaning. They could pose some great challenges, as they will require us to dig even deeper into our lives. If we dare to pay attention to the validity of these words in our lives, they will cause us to examine those parts of our lives we may have tucked away for the longest.

As an African Princess living in Diaspora, there are certain traditions and cultural beliefs that I am called to carry on. Likewise, just being a human being living in America, there are just some practices that one may be used to. These practices may or may not be healthy for us. They may range from eating very late at night, to speeding on the highway, or texting while driving, and substance abuse.

What unhealthy practices are you engaged in and what will it take to overcome them?

For us to live an amazing life, we need to be whole. Not only that, it is essential that we clean our hearts, clean our atmosphere and prepare for a heavenly download. Living an amazing life does not mean that bad things won't happen.

It simply means that you will address those issues and be in perfect peace, understanding that whatever it is, it's temporary, and will soon pass.

ACTIVITY – 2:
(1). What healthy practices are you engaged in?

(2a). Do you practice being joyful daily? If yes, how?

(2b). If no, why not?

____

____

____

____

____

____

____

____

____

____

____

____

____

____

____

____

____

____

____

____

____

____

(3). Do you seek peace at all cost with others around you?

____

____

____

____

____

____

____

____

____

____

____

____

____

____

____

____

____

____

____

____

____

(4). What attitude do you believe you need to remove from your way of living? Be very candid about it now. Only you can rescue YOU and it begins with telling the truth. You have the key to your own success locked inside of you. Your inner rock star is pleading to be released. Your genius will not be birthed until you provide an inviting atmosphere worthy of its presence.

———————————————————————
———————————————————————
———————————————————————
———————————————————————
———————————————————————
———————————————————————
———————————————————————
———————————————————————
———————————————————————
———————————————————————
———————————————————————
———————————————————————
———————————————————————
———————————————————————
———————————————————————
———————————————————————
———————————————————————
———————————————————————

(5). When there is unfinished business in your life… when you are allowing a certain behavior to take over your life, it is not conducive for your rock star to emerge. So what attitude must you be rid of for success to emerge? Are you a person who is overly jealous? Are you a self-saboteur? Do you lack faith? Are you an alcoholic or sex addict?

(6). What self-defeating thoughts occupy your mind, if any? What are your thoughts about wealth? Believe it or not, there are those who do not believe they should be wealthy. If you have had some failed venture, like I have, do you believe that you may never succeed?

Let's take a quick look at the word ***personnel*** in the dictionary definition shared earlier. This could also stand for those who surround you, that is, your *circle of influence.* So, here are my questions for you:

(7). Who have you included in your close circuit? What role are they playing on your success journey? Are they just there because you are used to them being there but there is really no value they bring to the relationship?

It is very important that you periodically evaluate those who surround you. There are dream breakers and dream makers. You must be able to identify who they are so that you are not crowding your core group with those who will drag you down!

____

____

____

____

____

____

____

____

____

____

____

____

More discussion on the **Dream Breakers and Dream Makers** can be found in the book, Release Your Vision Torch~ A Success Blueprint:
https://www.amazon.com/gp/bookseries/B017WCHMHW/#

For years, I crowded my core with the wrong people; those who appeared to be "it", but they were not producing anything of substance in my life.

Rather, I was giving more than I was receiving and we were all in the same boat, struggling with the same issues, praying over the same issues, and no one was breaking out of the cycle. After 30 years of drinking from the same old well, I finally got fed up, cleaned my heart and house, then launched out to begin doing things according to divine guidance and direction.

Now get this… once this happened, many of my "friends" quickly became "frenemies." Because they were not involved in the new things happening in my life, rather than just be happy for me, they pulled back and became jealous and bitter! Perhaps, this is what you may be experiencing now.

I share this because you must be prepared for such distractions once you have finally *aligned* yourself with your life purpose. The myth that you need these people to get to where you are meant to go is, of course, ridiculous. Those who are assigned to you in the season of your grace and favor will see what the creator is doing in your life and they will join in without envy.

CONCLUSION

It is never easy to remove those things or people we have become accustomed to, even when we know they are toxic. It is even more difficult to get rid of a habit… no matter how toxic it may seem... just ask any tobacco user.

For you to experience the fullness of who you were created to be, it is imperative that you examine the following:

(1). Acknowledge that you are not a perfect human being and it's OKAY!

(2). Acknowledge that because you are not perfect, you will always make mistakes. These mistakes mold and shape your character;

(3). Understand that you need others too. That is, your dream makers, to make things happen for you;

(4). Understand that you are a big factor in the manifestation of that which you desire. You must participate… therefore participate in your own success rescue™ or success recovery™;

(5). Participation will often begin with assessing the habits we have that can deter us from succeeding and getting rid of them.

This is covered in-depth in the masterclass. See you there.

Cleaning will require actions daily and may require repetition. "Rome was not built in a day," so do not expect to be done in one day. There will be times when events or occurrences will cross your mind and you will remember… what you do then is simply jot them down and add them to the list. As you make effort daily to address these "dead weights," it will get easier, particularly when you start seeing results falling into place in your life.

When our lives are a mess, it doesn't leave room for the real deal to appear… always remember that. If you insist on burdening your life with junk, that is what you will produce! Have you ever seen a farmer plant apples and harvest tomatoes? Therefore, what you eat is what you will digest, so be very careful to not allow negative things, thoughts, and deeds to fill your life. Once you have begun the process of cleaning, then it is time to dream a little. This will give us a break from the hard section and allow us to refocus on the reason why we have chosen to walk this discovery path.

YOUR NEXT STEPS

(1). Take this time to jot down all the ideas you have ever had. Remember, no idea or thought is silly.

(a). Those ideas that you considered a total bust... a failure;

(b). Those ideas where you enjoyed marginal success;

(c). Those ideas where you succeeded and considered it a slam-dunk! That is, when your success was incredible;

(d). Those ideas you have yet to accomplish.

All of these will require innovative thinking, lots of mediation, prayers, and focus. For more on this topic, see YOUR VISION TORCH™ series: The Book, Journal, and Quotation Book (Available on Amazon where all books are sold.

Your Vision is Worth the Effort.
It is worth the wait! **™**
It is worth all you are going through!
It is certainly worth the patience and diligent mastering
to deliver it safely.
Do You Believe?
~DR. PRINCESS FUMI HANCOCK

1. DISCOVER OR REDISCOVER YOUR PASSION

Curiosity is the seat of innovation and purpose discovery.

Hello there… Glad you are back reading the book. Many complain that they are not making headway in whatever it is they are desiring to do. While this may be a common complaint, it is vital that we also check ourselves, ensure that we have followed directions provided, and that we are doing everything we need to do on our part to succeed.

Due Diligence, Commitment, and Focus are Key Ingredients for Success.

As we take this journey together, can you make a commitment that you will give yourself the chance to "make it"; that you will completely be open to instruction; that you will stay engaged, and most importantly, you will participate in your own success rescue or recovery™.

Time awaits no man, so we must do what we are supposed to do today… right now, rather than later!

Now you are ready to replace the "dirt" you cleaned out of your house in the previous lesson. It is important that you replace that vacuum with something significant; something that will cause you to grow in the areas you desire whether it is in life, home, business and/or career.

The dictionary definition of "discover" alludes to finding something or someone unexpectedly. In other words, to locate, stumble upon, to show the presence of something hidden, shedding light upon a new discovery. Rediscover therefore means that which was lost before was now found. It points to rediscovering of a person or thing. I share these definitions with you, so that you can grasp where we are going with this chapter.

Many of you, if asked what you believe your purpose is, might know it succinctly; some may not be sure of what they are meant to be doing; others may be completely confused because of past experiences that have made them tuck away their vision. Either way, it is important that we discover who we are first before even attempting to ignite anything.

Here is the bottom-line, your true calling is innate. That is, your identity has always been there. It was designed and afforded to you right from your mother's womb. Before you were born, you were already pre-destined to be… *somebody*. For many, their life journey has really caused them to be misaligned with their purpose.

If I met you on the road and I were to ask you this question, "who are you?" what would your answer be? Would you tell me what you do for a living or would you describe yourself with words that transcend the job or title you hold? Would you be one of those whose life is completely wrapped up in their work or title? What then happens when the title or job ends? What will become of you? I have also seen people who bury themselves in taking care of a sick family member… they end up being caretakers for that family member and so their lives are meshed with that duty. What happens when that family member passes away? The answer is that they will have problems adjusting back to life. Or perhaps you are divorced and live daily with guilt of not spending enough time with your children due too long distance? Will you continuously beat yourself for something you had no control over?

I dare to tell you today that you are not your job, you are not your title, and you are certainly not what people call you. YOU ARE WHO YOU WERE CREATED TO BE FROM THE FOUNDATION OF THE EARTH. You are a mountain-mover™ and a valley-shaker™. Yes, you may have made mistakes; you may have gone through a bitter divorce, you may be single…all of those do not define you at the core of your being. You are more than a father, a mother, a sister, niece, nephew etc. Don't get buried in titles but look inside of yourself and this is what we are accomplishing on this journey.

YOUR DECLARATIONS:
I want you to declare the following:
(1). My job does not define me;
(2). My title does not tell people who I really am in the core of my being;
(3). If both should ever disappear, I will be still and understand that the Creator's plan for me, that is, my purpose in life, is bigger than my job or my title(s);
(4). I am who the Creator says I am… a Mountain-Mover™ and a Valley-Shaker™.

Discovering that you are a Mountain-Mover™ and a Valley-Shaker™ simply express the characteristics of who you were created to be. It is not attached to your job or titles but is anchored to your destiny. It speaks volumes… far beyond what a man can see with the naked eye. Sure, as parents, we are grateful for the gifts we were given in our children and as parents, we must value this responsibility and ensure that it is not threatened. In the same token, we must understand that disciplining our children are also our God given responsibility which we must ensure is not threatened by our self-inflicted guilt. How does this affect women who do not have children, whatever God has put in your hands, you are responsible for. Therefore, you must stand up and ensure that it is not threatened. Your duty lies in ensuring that you birth your destiny and not waste your pain.

> *When Identity Crisis Sets in,*
> *You Become Disconnected*
> *from Your Destiny.*

What blocks your view?

Many have not really seen themselves as a Mountain-Mover™ and/or a Valley-Shaker™. Therefore, an Identity Crisis sets in leading to a disconnection with their destiny.

When you understand the depth of those words, it will not only shed light on your destiny and destination, it will bring about a boldness that will ensure you conceive the habits necessary for birthing your true calling on fertile ground.

Do you know that the true definition of an entrepreneur is a Mountain-Mover™ and a Valley-Shaker™? Here is why, as a Valley Shaker™, you are tested by fiery trials. More so, challenges would often hit you and hit your family without warning. When the opportunity for growth arrives, you are bold like a lion, you understand the valley experience is temporary; you understand that it is not meant to kill you but to grow you; you totally get it that the experiences, life tools, and habits developed in the valley season are what promotes you to the mountain top. You cannot become a Mountain-Mover™ without you first becoming a Valley-Shaker™.

Sadly, many of us want to rush out of the valley experience, becoming half-baked leaders who are not ready to truly lead under any circumstances. It is important that you do not rush the process to avoid aborting your destiny before its scheduled delivery time.

How Do You Discover/ Rediscover Your True Identity?

We have heard of many who have committed suicide because they were unhappy with their lives. In fact, many had fame and money, yet there were things still missing. It is therefore imperative that we know that this journey is not just about how to make money or find purpose… it is equally about learning balance in our lives… and understanding that success is not just about money. While money is a pivotal part of our success journey, great health, awesome relationship with family, friends and peers, mental stability and, more importantly, living a *prosperous lifestyle* is important.

You accomplish all of these by first acknowledging that you are a Mountain-Mover™ and a Valley-Shaker™. An entrepreneur solves a problem for his or her customer thereby making him or her a Mountain-Mover™. A writer uses his or her pen, writing stories that elevate, inspire and motivate his or her readers. They move mountains and shake the valley on behalf of the readers; a nurse cares for his or her patient ensuring that the patient gets all necessary care while staying at the hospital; a medical doctor takes care of his patient, alleviates pain and ensures proper medical attention. In all these scenarios, they are shown to be Mountain-Movers™. When they are struggling to keep their businesses afloat, this can be described as part of the valley experience.

> *Your level of success will be dependent upon how you behave while in the valley.*

Once you have aligned your spirit with who you were already before you were born, that is, a Mountain-Mover™ and a Valley-Shaker™, then it really doesn't matter which vehicle you use to display who you are to the world. You may choose to be an author, a filmmaker or a fashion designer, and whatever avenue you choose to show the world your genius YOU WILL SUCCEED! Yes, you will have challenges and sometimes challenges that will cause you to doubt if you are doing the right thing… challenges that may cause you to even question if GOD was listening to you. You may lose relationships, money and other valuable things along the way. These are all part of your journey and what will make the journey eventually worth it. Our role is never to give up in the face of adversity.

Operating in your life purpose, as a Mountain-Mover™ and a Valley-Shaker™, qualifies you as a Word Changer and a World Leader. It is therefore not possible to change the world with your message without going through these phases of Success.

We often hear people saying how much they want to change the world, particularly those who are interested in Africa. The question is, are they willing to pay the price? Are they willing to do whatever it takes, legally of course, to ensure that they achieve success at that level?

This level of success often comes at a price? This does not make it unattainable but only that whoever desires to operate in the capacity of a World leader must be ready to work!

So, my question to you is this: Are you ready to do the work it takes to live an amazing life? Do you know just how worthy you are? Your enemies wake up every day, looking for ways to bring you down! Your worth and value is making Satan roam around seeking whom to devour. Your worth shines through everything you do and say. Understanding just how worthy you are will help you understand what I am about to share with you. I need for you to look at the little graph I have charted for you. Becoming a world leader takes courage, tenacity, commitment and hard work. It is equally evident that becoming a world changer entails going deep into the valley, shake yourself loose from all the baggage that comes at that level and soar to greater heights where you become a mountain mover™. As you begin to enjoy the perks that come with becoming a mountain mover, where you are being celebrated just because… As people begin to hear more about you through the works that you are doing, you become a world changer. A world changer looks beyond his or her own zip code and even go as far as globally ensuring that his or her efforts to bring about changes are implemented.

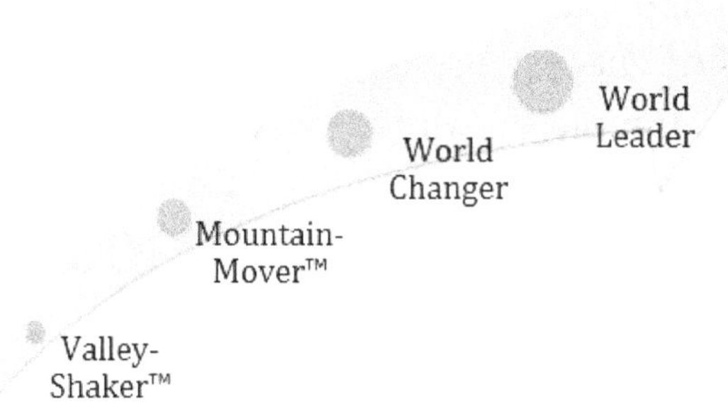

Now that you have established who you were created to be, that is, a Mountain-Mover™ and a Valley-Shaker™, what's next?

Time to Explore Your True Passion:
It is important that you begin to examine those gifting that come to you easily. Do not take this section of the book for granted. Take your time to really answer questions and whatever comes to you first is often the right answer.

(1). What do you think *passion* is meant to look like?

____

____

____

____

____

____

____

____

(2). What makes your spirit boil or gets you concerned when you hear about it? Do you believe there needs to be a solution to this? For example. John is always very passionate and upset whenever he hears about gang members fighting and shooting each other, even killing bystanders. John decides to become a police officer assign to areas where gangs fight the most. He believes helping to keep peace in impoverished areas within his community is his true calling.

Do you have your own personal example(s) or that of a family member/friend? Share it here.

> *One man's poison is*
> *another man's medicine.*

(3). What do you see yourself doing consistently that brings you satisfaction even if it is challenging for others?

____

____

____

____

____

____

____

____

____

____

____

____

____

____

____

____

____

(4). While it is true that there is nothing new under the sun, how we approach things will often differ. What is that special gift you have that no one else possesses or can translate like you?

(5). What would you consider doing even if you were not being paid for it? While writing is now a profession for me, it is a skill I can use even if not paid for it. I love to teach people how to turn their passion into profit. So I find myself constantly doing a balancing act between giving knowledge away and realizing that it is a gift to bless me financially too.

These are questions you must begin to ask yourself as you embark on discovery or should I say uncovering your true identity?

CAUTION: You are a problem solver and if what you have chosen is only benefitting you and not others, it will eventually fail.

Becoming a world leader is not about us but about the world entrusted to us to serve! The operative word, being *serve*. If your passion is self-serving, then it needs to be reviewed. You are a world changer because you are changing a component of the universe to ensure a better world for others. Whatever you do that has only "I" in it, will crumble eventually. On the other hand, if it serves people and solves problems for others, it is destined to succeed.

To discover or rediscover what our true purpose is, it is also important that we examine what it means to have a passion for something. Many people use interchangeably the words life purpose, true calling and/or passion. But truth be told, many times your passion will point to your true calling.

> *Words are incredibly powerful,*
> *as they can steer you to victory*
> *or defeat.*

As individuals, we all have an innate compass that directs us to what we really should be doing. Sadly, many ignore it because of their own self-designed desires. It is essential that you learn to hear that still, quiet voice, regardless of your own desires.

How then would you confirm exactly what you are meant to be doing?

You start by first examining your *Legacy.*

A *legacy* is anything left behind from the past. Free Dictionary Online further explains it as something (i.e. a gift, inheritance) handed down from an ancestor or a predecessor or from the past. Here is my question to you: If you had to write your own eulogy today, how would it read? What would you want people to remember you for? That is, what will your legacy look like? For instance, I, Dr. Princess Fumi Hancock, want to be remembered as an *Innovative Spirit-filled Global Vision Midwife*™, a *Life Rehab*™ *Ambassador* who helped other *Fearless Visionaries*™ and *Mountain-Movers*™ *birth their own legacies.*

WRITE YOURS NOW: (Keep to ONLY ONE SHORT SENTENCE).

Can you come up with a succinct description of your own legacy? Do it now! Make sure that both the beginning and the end of your sentence provides a very clear and concise description. More importantly, it must automatically paint a clear picture of the legacy you desire and answer the questions as to whether there is a personal meaning attached to it when others view it.

____

____

____

____

____

____

Here is a *Vision Nugget*™ for you today:

> *Your legacy always*
> *points to your true*
> *calling.*

Understanding your calling gives you your self-worth. Utilizing your calling to the maximum potential grows your self-esteem.

If you are looking to discover your true calling or passion or perhaps you want to rediscover your life purpose, the question you must candidly ask is: Does what you believe about yourself point to your legacy statement? If you have not yet found your life purpose, then write the legacy statement. This will clarify things for you. This question is pertinent for ascertaining your true calling or life purpose.

As an Entrepreneur, you are called to be a leader. The question now, as you begin to discover or rediscover your passion, is what type of leader would you be? As a leader, your staff is watching you meticulously and waiting on directions from you. Dependent on your actions, they too will either choose to commit to your vision or move out of the way.

As someone who dares to venture into entrepreneurship, we have established that you are a fearless visionary or perhaps you are venturing into a career path that you know is a calling for you. Bravo! However, there are different types of leaders. The goal here is to carefully consider the following and decide which one you are and what you need in your cycle to ensure your success. Your style of leadership will dictate your business or career outcome.

Which One Are You?

(1). ***Visionary***, by definition, is a person who is constantly thinking about or planning the future with innovation, creativity, inspiration and insight. Said leaders can discern visions in dreams. A visionary has original ideas about what the future will or could be. The ideas are clear and concise.

Often, these ideas may seem impossible for the season they have expressed them. They can therefore envision how the future should look like. A visionary is focused, always looking ahead, with a larger perspective, and delights in creating and finding new probabilities. What is most peculiar about a visionary is that once an idea comes into play, they are quickly on to another possibility. They are often the *heart* of the organization; an attribute that can be quite positive for the team and yet could also pose a threat to the team, if not well balanced.

The downside to becoming a visionary is that they are often referred to as dreamers who have the tendency to pay more attention to the future than their present obligations.

(2). An ***Executioner or Implementer*** is usually task oriented. They are the *hands* of the organization that get the job done! You can always count on them to bring the organization right back to the basics and account for what is necessary. They are sometimes narrow-minded and might find themselves unable to see the big picture, which the visionary sees. This can sometimes work to their advantage or it could be detrimental. The goal is to keep a good balance.

(3). The ***Cheerleader*** can sometimes be referred to as the greatest champion of the organization. This person is very passionate about the organization and would go to any length to ensure that others buy into the dream too. He or she represents the best of the organization and strives to always bring great awareness to the business.

They work diligently and have their hearts on the line too. They may not necessarily be very organized but when directed and given tasks, they excel.

(4). The ***Enforcer*** behind the organization is crucial to the success of said organization. The enforcer drives the organization to success. He or she ensures that company's objectives, mission, vision and goals are accomplished. He/she also makes sure that the policies and processes in place are adhered to. They understand what needs to be done and where the organization desires to go. They are very candid and factual and not afraid to deal with hard issues within the organization. They are self-assured, attentive, intense and methodical. Sometimes, this person may be too rigid, stifling the company he or she is working hard to bring to success. They could also be controlling and may want things a certain way no matter the cost. However, when hard decisions are necessary for implementation, you can always count on them to make them happen in record time.

(5). The ***Catalyst*** is a great leader, in that he or she initiates all plans. He or she is an excellent coordinator who sits comfortably between the Enforcer and Implementer. She/he is the heartbeat of the organization and can help balance things out, but more importantly, ensures that plans are put in place, deadlines are achieved, and morale of the team is high. They are great at offering recommendations or balancing deadlines that may have been designed by others versus realistic deadlines for projects at hand. They are also regarded as good active listeners, hands-on, accommodating and effective. However, when push comes to shove, they must figure out a way to ensure deadlines are met. What's great about *catalysts* is that they are reliable, competent and organized. They are also regarded as the guru of project management.

Again, what type of leader do you perceive yourself to be? The reason why you must answer that question candidly is that as you put together your success blueprint & your exit strategy for where you want to be, you must also start looking out for those that will appear in your circle of influence that can be positioned in the place of your weakness.

SUMMARY:
(1). Write down what you perceive as your legacy.

____

____

____

____

____

____

____

____

____

____

(2). How do you see yourself accomplishing this legacy?

(3). If you knew money was not an issue and you knew you would never fail, what would you do?

Our imaginations are incredibly powerful because they mirror our desires or our fears.

(4). Does your legacy point to what you believe you should be doing? That is, are they aligned? If they are, then bravo… let's move on to the next session ~*Ignite It!*

ASSIGNMENT #1:

I want you to just write what comes to you after reading this chapter. Don't think too hard. Just write. What have you learned from this chapter that you didn't know before? What have you been reminded of? How are you going to apply what you have learned in this chapter? What challenges do you anticipate encountering when applying this information to your daily activities?

____

____

____

____

____

____

____

____

____

There is so much more than meets the eye. *7 Days to Release Your Amazing Life*-masterclass will surely provide more resources and practical tools to help you dig deeper where Discovery or Recovery is concerned. The videos will bring to fore-front what we are discussing here. If you are like me, you want more than just this book. You want deeper answers; you need more practical tools, and you want step by step actionable plans to succeed here. So, log on to: www.storytellerbistro.com for *7 Days to Release Your Amazing Life.*

Regardless of what anyone says to you, you must be ready for change. No one can and will make the change you desperately desire in your life. Only you can!
DR. FUMI STEPHANIE HANCOCK

2. IGNITE YOUR PASSION

Unless you ignite your purpose, nothing will happen. It will only be mere discovery.

The various definitions of "Ignite" are very interesting. One definition is, to "catch fire or cause to catch fire". Another is "to arouse or inflame an emotion or situation". It is awesome that you have discovered or rediscovered your "inner genius" … that is, your passion or true calling. This only happens when you begin to value yourself… understand that you are worth all the effort and worth all the greatness you were meant to have. It is certainly my hope and desire that the last chapter has caused you to really take a candid look inside, to gain clarity thereby acknowledging that you are indeed special.

In the previous chapter, we concluded that if you are still struggling to know who you are; if you are battling to define your true calling or life purpose; then write yourself a legacy statement. This will point you to what you are supposed to be doing. Discovering your legacy equals unleashing your destiny and leaping into your life purpose. For someone who may still be struggling, your life purpose may need to be re-engineered, that is, refocused and *called out of retirement*. In other words, some of us have literarily parked your purpose and tucked it away. You have allowed the cares of this world to choke your destiny. Hence, it requires being called out of retirement and into the limelight.

Now that you have accomplished this wonderful discovery, you should be incredibly proud of yourself. Proud that you have discovered some wonderful things about you; excited that you know how valuable you are to this world and that the world would have lost a great visionary if you had allowed yourself to stagnate! You must, therefore, learn how to ignite it. I often tell my mentees that the world is waiting for their inner rock star to shine. So, I tell you that now too… the world is a better place because you are in it… you are a gem and a rock star that the world is waiting for. What you possess inside of you must be birthed so that the "tribe", who is destined to follow you, appears, but more importantly… that your teacher and mentor for that season appears too!

Many have told me on my periscope (@1PrincessofSub) and Facebook Live (@ I Am Princess of Suburbia TV broadcasts that fear is a big factor in unleashing or going after their passion or true calling. It is amazing how fear can kill our destinies, if care is not taken. What then should you do when fear takes over your thoughts? On my blog, http://www.yourinneryou.com, I mentioned how we hold ourselves back because of fear and if this debilitating *tendency* is not dealt with heads-on, it will destroy our best, most well-thought-out plans.

While I do not know what your core belief system is, for me, my love for God has been the key factor in overcoming fear. Please do not get me wrong, there are still times when I am afraid, particularly when I am asked or faced with making uncomfortable decisions.

MY PARADIGM SHIFT: *My Journey to Saudi Arabia*

Case in point, I remember when the opportunity came for me to consult in Saudi Arabia. This was a different scenery for me, one I was not accustomed to. Their culture, way of dressing, belief system, the country being primarily an Islamic nation… all these factors played a role in me first putting on the brakes to even see if the consulting work was what I needed in my life at that point.

Not only was I going to be out there, it was going to be for at least one year! Now, that was the kicker! I had travelled to many places in the world, but I have always returned home after few weeks. Next to my primary relocation to the United States of America from Africa, where I was born, this move was going to be significant. I needed a bigger "why", one that was greater than my fear of plunging into this opportunity. For six months, I was going back and forth with my decision. I prayed hard, meditated strongly and firmly, seek spiritually and mentorship counseling; then waited a little bit more. When I finally made the decision to accept the mission, the emotions were just indescribable when my plane landed in Saudi Arabia. Then another bout of fear creeped in… Would I succeed in this? Do I have what it takes to stay in the country and work this contract for at least one year? Is this move aligned with my overall corporate and personal goals?

That was not the end! Cascade of fear surged in when I finally found out that the team I was to lead was… well… challenging! I almost took my luggage, turned around and returned home! Someday, I intend to write a book on my journey to the Middle East. I believe it will be incredibly helpful for those who are on the fence about traveling and working abroad.

Many times, people wait for others to ignite their passion. We get lazy or perhaps too dependent on certain people to inspire, encourage, or even empower us. The truth be told, no one owes us anything. It is by sheer grace that the creator places encouragers in our paths. Because he or she was planted there to guide you, you must not stop taking the steps only you must take to succeed. Because I was assigned as your vision midwife, it does not mean you do not do anything on your end.

> *You are as GREAT, GOOD, or FAIR as what you put into your own DESTINY* JOURNEY.

Just recently, I had been teaching on "Jumping and /or Leaping" into ones' destiny and leaping out of relationships and other things that do not push us toward our life goal(s). Shortly thereafter, I was faced with putting action to my words - I had to leap out of a toxic business relationship, which paid very well but was taking me away from what I truly was meant to pursue. It was very difficult, and I almost began to second-guess myself that perhaps I had read it all wrong. Thank heavens my husband and one of my sisters were there to bring me back to reality. Do you have an accountability partner? If you don't, you may want to consider having one or perhaps finding a mentor that can help to ensure that you are on the right track at the right season.

Here is the deal; you must find whatever centers you. Valuable answers do not come in the middle of crisis. You must cocoon yourself in peace and love, and then allow the divine one, the creator of the universe, to pilot your life while you co-pilot.

Igniting signals your need for a torch, or a match, to light the fire and then torch that which is within. When you ignite your life's mission, you are highlighting your life's purpose. Many of us are missing key ingredients for torching our destiny fire. We may be missing the torch itself, or we are out of position, or don't even have a purpose to torch. I once told a story in one of my books about an Olympic torch bearer. It is very interesting when you watch them prepare to carry the torch to where they need to set the fire ablaze. As they run toward the sacred place, they hear the cheers of people, but they are completely focused on where they are going. Though they enjoy the applause of admirers, they do not allow it to become a distraction. Sometimes, you see them turn slightly to acknowledge the raving fans, and then quickly turn back, re-focusing on their destination. As they get closer, the exhilaration in the air becomes tangible, and so is the responsibility placed on them to ensure a successful lighting! They are completely focused, and I can imagine them drowning the noises around them to insignificance so all they can see is the Olympic flame ahead.

A mentee once asked me a question, what is the difference between being impromptu … moving out of season and creating opportunities? This was a great question that needed much meditation. After much deliberation, I came to believe that there is truly a difference. One is completely blessed and the other not blessed. One is appointed and because it is an appointment time, help, resources… everything needs to show up. The former, that is, moving out of season, you are constantly find yourself pulling to make things happen. There is nothing wrong with being resourceful, but it is important to never get ahead of our creator. If the "opportunity" you are creating is encouraging you to skip the process needed for that path you have chosen, that is you moving out of alignment.

Every journey has its processes.

You cannot practice as an Advanced Nurse Practitioner or a Physician without undergoing the proper training. In fact, putting up your shingle without certification is criminal! Unfortunately, there are some business or career paths that are not so clear cut. Because we have been divorced before, then we believe it automatically qualifies us to start counseling others in that arena. While this may have been the first step to steering you in that direction, it doesn't necessarily mean that is your destination. What will either confirm if this is truly your path or not are the processes in place. Until you embrace the processes it takes to truly be qualified both spiritually, emotionally, physically, you cannot claim that path.

This is where the rubber meets the road for many of us: life coaches, incredible amount of business strategists, many personal growth strategists, personal brand strategists... and the list goes on. However, if we were to truly count the number of people who were really called to these areas, it's not a lot. When I look at the nursing profession, many are nurses today because they felt that calling. They knew they were created to care for others in that capacity. If asked if they had a second plan to nursing, they would say no. I know a few in my family. Even in my family, where we do have four nurses and another one in training as I write, I cannot truly be certain that all 4 of us were called to nursing. Though I believe that we were all called to the caring profession... the avenue is what I often question. Though we all excelled at it, it still did not mean we were all called to it. Out of the 4 of us, only one went straight into nursing. She never did anything else and never wanted to be anything else but that. Today, she is an advanced nurse practitioner with cardiology as her area of expertise. She excels brilliantly in it, thrives exceptionally, and would not mind working for others just doing what she loves best... nursing. One of us had her degree in Adult Education and it didn't matter what she specializes in, that is, what subject she was teaching, she excelled at it. So, while nursing is not her first love, she has grown to love it and teaches it too. She too has now become an advanced nurse practice who is also expanding her scope to include Midwifery. The other two include me and a younger sister who frankly have worn two hats most part of our lives.

For me, I am a master storyteller! This is what I know I was put on this earth to fulfill... to use the art of storytelling to change lives. I accomplish this through writing, speaking, hosting TV/Radio, and making inspiring movies. Where does nursing come in? I am glad you asked. I often tell people that just like I cared for patients when I was a floor nurse, I do the same with my characters. Frankly, I believe that nursing has made my writing incredibly rich. I am constantly drawing from my experiences on the floor and as an Advanced Nurse Practitioner, Mental Health (Psych.), it is so helpful in dealing with my mentees as well as in creating poignant courses… ones, people will be proud to participate in without hesitation. While some may look at the fact that I do have post graduate degrees in Communication Arts (Writing for the Media Arts) and Advanced Nurse Practice far from each other; to me… it is much closer. It is an opportunity to influence both fields in such a positive way. On the other hand, I have a sister who is alright with working in the nursing field, but her passion is not even close. She loves the fashion industry and just blossoms in that field.

Whatever your passion is, you must learn to ignite it even when all odds are against you. When it looks like you are exhausted and there is no way out, it is your zeal for that calling that will keep you going. It will strengthen you when you are weak; pull you up when you are feeling down; cause you to excel even in drought seasons. This is what happens when you do it right: When everyone is going through dry spots, you are blooming with no reasonable explanation.

What are the necessary ingredients you need to ignite your passion/true calling?

It's going to require courage, determination, and focus… a willing and believing heart and, most of all, faith that regardless of what you seem to hear or think, you will succeed. Just recently, I had the most incredible experience of my life. While in Saudi Arabia, one of a member of my team talked me up and nominated me to speak on TEDx Talk (https://youtu.be/IjFPKUSN3NQ) /

(https://youtu.be/k8bVsCDTEfo). You must understand why this meant the most to me. Here I was, a black African-American (Nigerian descent) on a stage that's never been graced by a black person before: 2018 TEDx Al Anjal National Schools. Need I say, I was very pleased with the outcome… and they were too. What were the lessons I took away from this experience? That we must always remain open and BE READY for opportunities. I learned that these opportunities may not always come in the gift box we expect. What if I had said no to the opportunity of going to Saudi Arabia? What if when I eventually got there, I mistreated the young lady who nominated me? It is important that we treat people right as we do not know the role they may yet play in our growth. While I understood that invariably I may have been nominated in the US at some point, the fact remains that I will never have been the first African American or an African princess or better yet black person to have graced that platform in AlHasa, Saudi Arabia.

Affirmations are a great way to ignite your true calling. They ensure that you have your success in front of you every time you say them. Look at it this way, the more you say these affirmations, the more they become part of you and the possibility increases that you will truly take them on as part of your belief system.

> *You were born to succeed; you were made for greatness; designed for victory and called to a higher ground where all things are possible. But, it is ultimately your choice what you do with your calling.*

Here are some affirmations to help you torch your life purpose (Create What You Say & Conceive!)

Today right now and right here:

I will *Release My Inner Rock Star and Jump* into My God-given Destiny;

I will *Release My Inner Rock Star and Jump* into Blessings;

I will *Release My Inner Rock Star and Jump* into Fruitfulness;

I will *Release My Inner Rock Star and Jump* into the Greatness I already am;

I will *Release My Inner Rock Star and Jump* into Immeasurable Favor;

I will *Release My Inner Rock Star and Jump* into great Health;

I will *Release My Inner Rock Star and Jump* into Abundant Rain of God's Mercy;

I will *Release My Inner Rock Star and Jump* into Endless Joy;

I will *Release My Inner Rock Star and Jump* into God's Goodness;

I will *Release My Inner Rock Star and Jump* into Profitable and Dynamic Ideas;

I will *Release My Inner Rock Star and Jump* into Divinely Orchestrated Promotion;

I will *Release My Inner Rock Star and Jump* into Financial Release

I will *Release My Inner Rock Star and Jump* into Breakthrough;

I will *Release My Inner Rock Star and Jump* Over Failure to Launch;

I will *Release My Inner Rock Star and Jump* Over Obstacles;

I will *Release My Inner Rock Star and Jump* Over Stagnation;

I will *Release My Inner Rock Star and Jump* Over Set-Back;

I will *Release My Inner Rock Star and Jump* Over Sickness and Incurable Diseases;

I will *Release My Inner Rock Star and Jump* Over Frustration & Regrets;

I will *Release My Inner Rock Star and Jump* Over Abject Poverty;

I will *Release My Inner Rock Star and Jump* Over Bad News;

I will *Release My Inner Rock Star and Jump* Over Put-down;

I will *Release My Inner Rock Star and Jump* Over the Shackles of the Enemy;

I will *Release My Inner Rock Star and Jump* Over the Burdens and Yoke of the Enemy.

Questions to Ponder Upon:

(1). What do you want to create right now? Don't be hindered by financial status. *Just dream.*

____

____

____

____

____

____

____

Recommended Resource:
Holding Back the Fears: *Conquering Fears Part 1*
http://www.yourinneryou.com/holding-back-the-fears-conquering-fears-part-1/

In this season, I am watching GOD carefully selecting my circle and those who may have entered via way of highway robbery, GOD is kicking them out! If this is happening to you, don't fret! You are being prepared for a bigger platform!
DR. PRINCESS FUMI HANCOCK

3. LAUNCH YOUR PASSION

Unless you ignite your purpose, nothing will happen. It will only be mere discovery.

In the last chapter, *Ignite It,* we discussed at length, how to Ignite Your Legacy, that is, your true calling or what some call life purpose. In addition, we also discussed the importance of ensuring that your legacy catches fire. In other words, I provided some questions, which I hope to have ultimately empowered you into igniting whatever it is that you desire to do.

> *If no one will open the door for you, make the decision to break the doors down or create your own door and work diligently, that is, on a consistent basis.*

Let's start this section by celebrating your success in igniting your passion. We will also recap what I stated at the very beginning of one of my books, *365 Days to Release Your Vision~* Wise Quotes for Life, Home, and Business; I discussed how you did not find your calling, but that your calling finds you and compels you daily to act.

Often, this action is prompted by your "why." In other words, finding your "why" will help to encourage you in times of frustration. Hopefully, the last few sessions have helped you in not only finding your "why" but also igniting it. The action you take is what is referred to here as the *Launch Your Passion* phase. What good does it do when your light is burning so brightly, and you sit on it? Here, I will teach you and provide some thoughts to consider that will help you to not only launch successfully, but launch safely and fearlessly.

Sadly, this is an area where many, fall short myself included. Together, let's tear the veil. To be frank, I have started many businesses that invariably failed. By the same token, I have also started businesses that were successful… case in point, my day care centers in New York. I have been through the spectrum and understand when people are frustrated seeing that they continue to experience the failure to launch syndrome. In retrospect, many have failed right at the point of launching. This is known as the *ceiling syndrome*™ where you are at the point of succeeding, you can breathe the air of success then suddenly, everything falls apart! For me, I was great at discovering my passion, igniting it but when it came time to launch, I failed miserably. Therefore, I am the right one to show you what to do and what not to do, to ensure your own success. I always tell my mentees; your success does not have to be a 30-year run like mine! Having a mentor, virtual or face-to-face, would have saved me a great deal of pain.

To launch your passion, it is essential that you are clear about your message to the world. Not only that, your legacy statement should be one that you are able to say from the heart; particularly when asked in a fast-paced environment. This statement must be delivered in seconds. Launching your passion or business means that you understand the inner workings of said business or passion and you are the best person to executive it. You are not only tapping into the ordinary, but now into the extraordinary realm, where you are meant to be.

As a creative person with an entrepreneurial spirit, I am often tempted to want to touch every aspect of my business. In fact, I love to multitask. While this is a great asset, it can also hinder the progress of your evolving passion or business. Before you decide to launch your business or passion, it is important that you lay a solid foundation. I always tell my mentees to learn to stay in their lane. In other words, it is important that you outsource the areas where you are the weakest. For instance, if you are weak in marketing, then you are not doing yourself any favors by attempting to market your product/service on your own.

There are four very significant assigned positions for a business to be successful: The Chief Executive Officer (CEO), Chief Financial Officer (CFO), Chief Marketing Officer (CMO), and Chief Operating Officer (COO); a great lesson I learned from my own mentors. As a startup, it is very likely that one or two persons may be taking on more than one role.

Let's use the Princess of Suburbia® as an example to bring home my point. At the startup phase of the brand, I found myself taking on all the C-level roles. For that reason, the brand was not growing as fast as it could have. I got extremely tired and found myself running in circles. I was not really making money, but I was spending a lot. With mentorship, I have learned to simply acknowledge that handing parts of my responsibilities over is not a sign of weakness but a show of strength, discipline, and a character trait of a successful empire builder. Hence, I quickly handed over the COO responsibilities to someone else, the CMO to another viable company, the CFO to my current accounting company, while I maintain the CEO position.

I know many are probably wondering if this would take too much money to hire capable people for those positions. Do not fret. YOU HAVE OPTIONS. One is presenting a percentage of your business to those who you believe have the funds and are willing to wait until the company begins to make money. If you are not comfortable with giving a percentage of your company away for expensive labor, then you must figure out how to make these part-time roles for limited wages.

Launching dictates that you are ready to push through and soar. It means that you are ready to attract your teacher. Your mind must align with your greatness on which you must be clear, since you are the one who began this journey.

Entrepreneurship or Intrapreneurship (i.e. Professional-entrepreneur) is not for the faint at heart. However, it requires tenacity and commitment to your cause. People will never believe in your cause unless you show your excitement and commitment to that cause. It really doesn't matter the product or services you are looking to launch, you must be dedicated in both the good and the bad times, because bad times will surely come.

Business will experience ups and downs, but you owe it to yourself, to not only learn from the best, but also be prepared in every way possible.

Another step you may want to consider is finding a mentor who can help you, step by step through your plans. This pivotal step is a gamechanger! As you venture into whatever you are attempting to do, situations will arise that you will need to seek counsel. My mentor holds me accountable! They do not implement strategies for me, but they point me in the right direction. This is the role of a Vision Midwife™.

Here is a ***MUST-HAVE LIST*** before you launch into your newly ignited life purpose:

(1). Are you ready? I mean physically, mentally, and/or emotionally? Is your team ready, no matter how small they are? Even if it is just team "YOU".

* Pray *Meditate *Ensure your alignment with the Creator.

(2a). If you are proposing to launch a business, have you taken care of the business aspect? For example, registered your business either as a Sole Proprietorship, Limited Liability Company/Partnership, or Incorporation? *My Wisdom Nugget* where this is concerned:

*If you are just starting out, consider being a sole proprietorship and wait till you start earning money before you consider any other entity. Once you start making money, I would advise you to speak with an accountant or attorney to see what the next best step is for you. At any rate, it's how you eat an elephant, one bite at a time. I share this because of the grievous mistakes I made where I went straight to Incorporation, ended up spending so much money while making nothing. Seek counsel on this please.

(2b). Have you handled all the tax requirements for your state?

(3). Do you have an asset or something proprietary that needs to be trademarked? Money comes out of proprietary assets. For example, the course you are currently taking is an asset for me. The books that I publish, and sell are assets to me.

List your assets that you desire to launch. Hopefully, you have worked on the list during the Ignite it phase, as you must know what they are to even ignite them, right?

Depending on what you are presenting to the public, there are some assets you can just copyright while you work on trademarking them. In other words, you can copyright them and begin to disseminate them, while you wait on the trademark. For information on Trademarks:

http://www.uspto.gov/trademarks-application-process/search-trademark-database

(4). Are you presenting yourself as a brand to your tribe? This is critical to showcasing your uniqueness. It is best to carve it out from day one. For example, I have always been known as the Princess of Suburbia® from day one. When I launched my brand, I had no money to hire an attorney. So, I took the somewhat harder road of doing it myself:

http://www.uspto.gov/trademarks-application-process/search-trademark-database

The application was rejected the first time, as I had to send additional information to prove I had been using that name for a while. Ultimately, I was given the trademark. If I did it, so can you! However, if you have the resources to hire an attorney, then, go that route. My trademark came out after a little over one year of using the name: The Princess of Suburbia®. So, if you are looking at trademarking a name or a slogan, begin using it with a ™ at the end. This will be your proof of use.

Here is an advantage of branding yourself and /or business: the possibility of duplicating yourself for higher income and opportunities for residual income. Just recently, an International Fashion House approached me to license my brand name. I did and it and the financial deal I cut with them was marvellous!

My Wisdom Nugget where this is concerned:

*First check to make sure that no one is trademarking or has trademarked what you seek to trademark. You accomplish that by searching the database: http://www.uspto.gov/trademarks-application-process/search-trademark-database

*This does not preclude you from finding an attorney to place on retainer.

(5). Now that you know that the name or slogan you want to use is free and clear where trademark is concerned, have you picked the domain name (URL) too?

There are several sites where you can pick up URLs at reasonable pricing: Blue host & Go daddy are the two sites I use. You are also able to create new websites at Wordpress.com and Wix.com. To upgrade your website for the future, I would advise you to go to Wordpress.com/wordpress.org. I have used both.

My Wisdom Nugget where this is concerned:

*Whatever you do, you must create a way of increasing your mailing list. Your mailing list is money!

I currently use aweber.com and Leadpages.net for landing pages. I have seen people use Mail Chimp to start with. It has a free service component.

(6). You have a legacy statement, right? Is it aligned with what you desire to accomplish with your business or professional life?

(7). Have you created a cash flow, which maps out what you hope to earn by the end of the year? Work with whoever you have assigned to be your CFO and, if it is you, then you need to be crystal clear on the cash flow for the year. Your mentor should be able to assist you with this.

(8). Have you mapped out your Marketing Strategy with your CMO? Perhaps it is just you taking up that role… what marketing plan have you mapped out for your products or services?

My Wisdom Nugget where this is concerned:

*Once you have mapped this out, it is easier to find a virtual assistant or, better yet, an intern to run with it and make it work.

* This should include a free product or service that can be used during the marketing campaign. For example, it could be something you could send via email. It does not have to cost you anything but time to put it together. e.g. a resource book for your industry.

(9). You mapped out a Media/Public Have Relations Strategy? Or perhaps you have hired a PR person to bring awareness to your brand.

(10). Have you examined your list of organizations and influencers in your area of expertise?

(11). What other things must you put in place that is unique to your area of expertise or your business etc.?

(12). Have you found an accountability partner?

(13). Do you have a mentor? If not, check out my mentoring programs: send your email to: successlaunchbp@theprincessofsuburbia.com

Once you have painstakingly gone through the list, you are ready to launch safely and fearlessly. When you go over this list and some steps are lacking, please take your time to ensure your success.

> *Never devalue your humble beginnings.*
> *They are the seasons of your life that add*
> *character to your existence and provide you*
> *with wings to fly high. So, appreciate the*
> *seasons when you crawl or leap on one leg*
> *and be grateful for times when you walk on*
> *your own two feet.*

RESOURCES:

What is in your cash-flow plan? Create a cash flow for the whole year up to two years as forecast.

E.g. 2017 Plan: Use Excel Spreadsheet for easy access and visibility.

- **Total Income**

**Total income (sales) - G&A-Cost of goods sold-Sales and marketing costs=profit Cash on Hard Beginning of the month

Product/Service sales (100%)

**List each product/service in order of % in sales cash from Investors (If applicable)

Anticipated # of consumers/ sales

- **Total Expenses**

Cost of Production of Product/Services Other Expenses:

**Legal

**Accounting

**Office expenses (listed individually)

Payroll

Marketing Expenses

Loan Payments (If applicable)

- **List Your Assets**

This can be as detailed as necessary. Please implore your Bookkeeper/ Accountant.

PS: Because of the in-depth nature of this part, those who are enrolled in my mentoring One-on-One program will have direct access with me and are able to work on this with my supervision. I am looking forward to that. Details of my mentoring programs can be accessed at:
www.storytellerbistro.com

Please understand that your cash flow is the "bread and butter" of your organization and it cannot be ignored or neglected.

We must choose to be an active participant in our own journey. Just wishing things will not make them happen. Activate your life today by taking massive action.
~DR. FUMI HANCOCK

4. LIVE OUT YOUR PASSION

We have the power to change our atmosphere.

We live in a world, full of dramatic events. Many are looking to gain wealth in uncanny ways and impatience has become the order of the day. Some say this is the microwave age where people want things now or never! During this drama, after you have worked so hard to launch your dream, you owe it to yourself to live in the moment. That is, to enjoy your success and hard work; to watch YOU, Inc. soar like an eagle.

I am sure this is not your first time of hearing that life is way too short. A little while back, my family was faced with the most difficult situation. It was four days before the New Year. I received a heart wrenching call from Africa. One of my older brothers who travelled home on vacation was in a ghastly accident, while he was being taken to the airport to board his flight back to the United States where he had lived for over forty years! Not only that, my other brother who was sitting in the front ended up in a coma while his wife who sat at the back of the car died. There is always a thanksgiving opportunity in the middle of tragedy. My second brother came out of the coma. But the deaths of two family members in one day were just unimaginable. When something like this happens, there is the tendency to question everything one has believed to be true about God; one may even be tempted to ask "why". My family's' decision was not to question the Creator but to be thankful for the life they lived and the legacy they left behind.

> *The way you write your story will determine your outcome. Write with intention and curiosity.*

How then do you live your purpose?

David Bowe, a Rock Icon Dies at 69! News media blasted all over their broadcasts, both nationally (in the US) and internationally. While the news was indeed sad that the world had lost a great man, I was rather intrigued by the legacy he left behind.

Can you read the blog first? David Bowie, a Legacy left behind!

http://www.yourinneryou.com/david-bowie-dies-at-69-a-legacy-lesson-for-all-princess-of-suburbia-chimes-in/

Living your purpose means living your legacy and ensuring that your revealed legacy is mapped out. Right now, there should be no question as to what your legacy statement is. In addition, there should not be any question as to how to ignite and launch your passion. At this present time, this session is helping you to live life full no matter how busy you may get. The goal is to leave life empty!

It is important that you live a balanced life! Do not be like those who work so hard that they do not even enjoy the fruits of their labor. That is not success. Success means being a well-rounded person, not necessarily perfect, but one who understands the meaning of success.

You live by constantly reminding yourself about the legacy you desire; the one you have written down and how you are going to bring it to fruition. No one is promised tomorrow, but we have today to work with. We must therefore ensure that we are living life full health-wise, financial wise and relationship-wise.

When you live your legacy, you are essentially calling out your inner genius for optimal success.

Here are 7 ways you can Call Out Your Inner Genius for Optimal Success:

(1). Making a deliberate decision to live out your legacy, unapologetically.

(2). Not settling for anything less than the greatness that you are.

(3). Allowing your life to speak volumes and change your world.

(4). Paying your blessings forward daily.

(5). Choosing not to allow toxic people infest or invade your fruitful space. This will take discernment and obedience.

(6). Saying a categorical "YES" to Destiny, despite what the environment may dictate.

(7). Be Bold, Strong, Committed, Loyal to your cause. In addition, determined to make an intentional choice to receive the purpose that has already found you.

> *You are the architect of your own change. Quit waiting on someone to make the change you ought to make for yourself.*

Take a hard look at every aspect of your lifestyle:
Relationship(s): Healthy or not healthy (Yes/No). If no, what will you do to make the necessary changes?

We also must be realistic where relationships are concerned, as there is a season for everything under the sun. We must therefore learn how to discern who is expected to be in your circle for the season you are operating in.

My book, Release Your Vision Torch: *A Blueprint for Success* does a great job at expanding on this: http://www.amazon.com/gp/bookseries/B017WCHMHW/

____

____

____

____

____

____

____

____

____

____

____

Physical: Healthy or not healthy (Yes /No)

What do you have to work on? Your weight? Are you battling an illness? What plans do you have in place to live a healthy life?

Emotional: How would you rate your emotional stance? (10 being extremely great, 0 being extremely poor) What plans do you have in place to ensure that you continue to be emotionally balanced?

____

____

____

____

____

____

____

____

____

____

____

____

____

____

____

____

____

____

____

A while back, I wrote a Wisdom Nugget on one of my blogs. I also included this in my book as Wisdom Nugget # 5. In it, I discussed 7 ways you can steer your vision without fear. When you are healthy, fear becomes an effective tool in your hands and not a destructive one.

Summation

There are steps you can begin taking today to ensure that you continue to live your passion, regardless of what your environment dictates.

(1). Believe that you are operating in your greatness and never allow anyone to undermine that.

(2). Understand that life is full of highs and lows, but we have the tenacity and God given strength to push through and maintain our greatness.

(3). There is a season for everything… a season for breakthrough; a season for breakups; a season of business hiccups and a season where you soar incredibly high. We must therefore be prepared.

(4). Never lose track of the gift with which you have been endowed and regardless of what happens around you, stay in your own lane. In addition, hone your craft and be the best that you can in your own lane.

(5). You must Focus! Focus! Focus! You will never get better at what you do not take the time to practice.

(6). Daily, you must make an intentional decision to take massive action towards your goals. You will conquer the mountain, one step at a time.

(7). Be vigilant to ensure that you are aligned with the persons divinely assigned to you in the season you are operating in.

(8). Take time to constantly revisit your legacy statement. This will ensure that you continue to walk in the path necessary to fulfill your dreams.

> *Regardless of what it looks like, you are a great warrior. Don't judge your destination by what appears to undermine who you truly are today.*

*Fear will handicap you, if allowed to fester in your life.
Whatever vision you may have,
it will always require an action minus fear.*
DR. PRINCESS FUMI HANCOCK

5. TURN YOUR PASSION INTO PROFIT

Curiosity is the seat of innovation and purpose discovery.

This phase is what you have been working toward either as an entrepreneur or professional intrepreneur. This is what you have hoped for… that your passion will one day generate profit (or more income) for you. Remember, at some point you must pay your blessings forward. What better way than to have more than enough to be a blessing financially to others?

A while back, one of my sisters called me. She wanted to share a revelation she had received that morning. I was eager to listen, as she sounded incredibly excited about the revelation. While many of us sit on the fence, trying to figure out if we are ready to jump into that which we are called, it is important that we make the decision, get off the fence and just spring into it! A parked car will always remain parked, until the owner puts the key into the ignition, turns it on and drives it. Likewise, it doesn't matter how prepared you are on paper, this phase is where you put action to your words and begin to work the plan diligently to ensure that what you have predicted in your cash flow happens!

The revelation is this: That we are called to do what we love. That is, we are called to live out our life purpose. There is money in "love". This means that when you do what you love, you are constantly sharing love and when you are doing that, the love attracts wealth to you! Let's look at this in a practical way.

Oprah is loved because she extends her love to her viewers as she shares what she loves, that is, what she knows she has been called to do… impacting the world at large by offering ways they can better their own lives. She presents this by way of interviews, book clubs, movies, talk shows, and now her OWN network.

Life lesson: The more she shares her love, the wealthier she gets. And her wealth seems to come effortlessly, though not without a few hiccups. But more importantly, she is enjoying the ride and taking others along with her. This is what it will take to turn your passion into profit.

The dilemma many have is the difficulty in thinking outside of the box. How do we monetize what we love so much that we are willing to give it away for FREE, with no strings attached? How do we shift our mindset to understanding that though you love this passion, you can make money from it? Many even ask questions if their passion or true calling is supposed to be making them money, for example, someone in ministry.

Here is the truth: Regardless of what you are doing, be it a ministry, writing, whatever; your passion will require you to engage your entrepreneurial spirit to make it successful (even if you are running a non-profit organization as this is business too or climbing the professional ladder). What separates a successful ministry/professional/business from those not so successful are management and the mindset of a leader. This is the same for any other venture, including being an author. Therefore, you must ensure that you are fully engaged in the process, ditch your fear, excommunicate procrastination, and be determined to put in the work!

> *Focus is the key to igniting ones' calling. You cannot afford to get carried away by distractors… especially those who will praise you even when you are going in the wrong direction.*

Once you have dealt with your mindset; and understand that even a ministry must be managed like a business (the only difference is that you are using other peoples' money to run the ministry), then it is time to put all of YOU into it and make it work!

Remember this:

Where there is no vision, it doesn't matter what you are trying to do or become, NOTHING WILL WORK! Your life journey must start with a vision. Often, our vision may be obscured due to life challenges but for those who persevere and pull through challenges, Victory awaits at the end.

Monetizing Your Passion:

Regardless of what your passion is, know that you can monetize it. It is only a matter of asking few questions that can point you in the right direction.

There is nothing like using a clear example to show how you can monetize your own passion:

Jamie is an illustrator. How will she monetize her passion as an illustrator?

There are fundamental questions that must be answered to steer you in the right direction:

(1). Besides illustrating, what does Jamie love to do?
Loves to *Speak& Teach* Loves to *Write* Loves to *Run His Own Business*

There are 4 avenues Jamie can begin looking at to turn her passion for illustration into profit. Let us explore:

(i)(a). Public Speaking

(i)(b). Coaching/Mentoring

(ii). Write a Book/Articles

(iii). Run Her Own Small Business where she is hired to illustrate and where she employs other artists to work for her.

Having identified 4 possibilities for Jamie, she must now **place them in order of preference and conviction.**

This is where Jamie must be authentic with her feelings and what comes first for her. Hopefully, previous lessons have taught Janie how to stay true to "self". That is, how to stay in her lane by being original. After much thought, here is what Jamie came up with:

Jamie's Legacy Statement:

I want to provide *practical tools and tips* to *Illustrators,* ready to take their life passion to the *Next Level of Success,* *yielding Global Awareness, Impact & Financial Breakthrough.*

Jamie's Life Purpose:

I was born to birth the next generation of world-changing illustrators.

How Will Jamie Accomplish Her Legacy Statement and/or Life Purpose?

1st Priority Coaching/Mentoring

2nd Priority Public Speaking

3rd Priority Write a Book/Articles for relevant magazines

4th Priority Start a Small Business where she employs other illustrators. Jamie, in this instance, can monetize her passion through several avenues:

Products & Services:

(1). She can provide coaching/*mentoring programs*:

Virtual & One-on-One Mentoring Programs (her audience can be the following: newbies, veteran illustrators who are looking to go back into the market, and/or those who are currently working in the field and just need to advance their knowledge in new techniques)

*Virtual Mentoring: e.g. e-Learning Courses

*Skype Meetings

(2). She can offer to **speak** at conventions/ organizations/ schools for illustrators, etc.

(3). **Write a Book** for Illustrators. As a speaker, this will generate additional revenue.

*Jamie can also agree to write articles and find opportunities to be a paid columnist. Another option is to create a blog, build her tribe and sell ad space on her blog site.

(4). All the above are income-generating assets for Jamie. If she chooses to just manage those, she will be fine. However, if the demand is there, she can also decide to start a small Illustration, Arts & Graphics company, which provides affordable services to small business owners.

While I will love to really delve into each of these areas, it is almost impossible to tell you how to map yours out, as there are other extenuating circumstances that must be taken into consideration. However, the blueprint provided here will work for any business or profession, if it is adhered to studiously. In addition, this blueprint can be followed during a mentoring session. Mentoring will not only provide more time to delve into each component of your moneymaking asset, but it will provide an in-depth, one-on-one expert close-up at your blueprint.

To get you started on the path of turning your passion into profit, this is your moment to draw a skeletal vision map of your empire. Let's begin:

(1). Who Are You?
HINT: You are a Mountain-Mover™, a Valley-Shaker™, & World Changer.

____

____

____

____

____

____

____

____

____

____

____

(2). What is Your Legacy Statement?

HINT: You should have written it in one of the earliest lessons. It must not be longer than one to two sentences; one sentence is preferable. Rewrite Now.

____

____

____

____

____

____

____

(3). What is Your Life Purpose?

HINT: You should have written it in one of the earliest lessons. Rewrite Now.

____

____

____

____

____

____

____

____

(4a). How will YOU Accomplish Your Life Purpose and/or Legacy?

HINT: Place in order of Priority and/or Preference

____

____

____

____

____

____

____

____

____

____

____

____

____

____

____

____

____

____

____

____

____

____

(4b). If you have listed more than 3, then place here the first three that you will focus on.

____

____

____

____

____

____

____

____

____

____

(5). Do you see an alignment in any of the three? That is, do they complement each other or are they independent of each other? Clarify.

Hint: **Jamie's Case Study**

1st Priority Coaching/Mentoring

2nd Priority Public Speaking

3rd Priority Write a Book/Articles for relevant magazines

4th Priority Start a Small Business where she employs other illustrators. She can also duplicate herself, i.e. her business model by teaching other illustrators who desire to start a coaching/mentoring business.

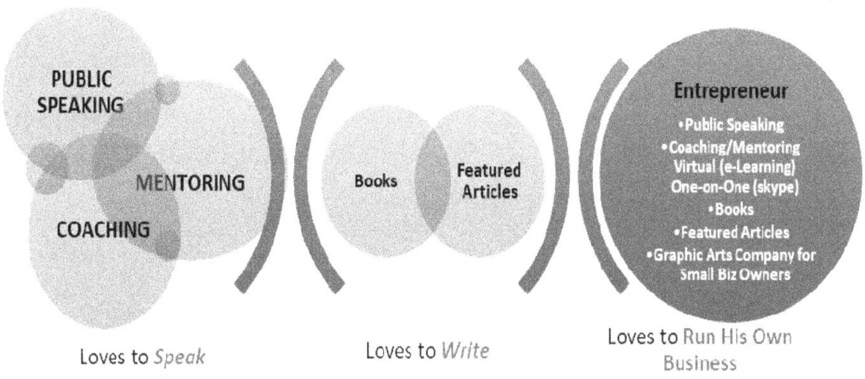

Now that you have determined all of these, draw up your prosperity and business plans to make your success manifest.

Now, on to your own assignment:
What alignment do you notice in your first 3 priorities? ***If you do not see any, then you need to rework this.*** *Usually where the 3 priorities meet is where innovation collides.*

____

____

____

____

____

____

____

____

____

Let's take a look at where innovation collides in your order of priorities:

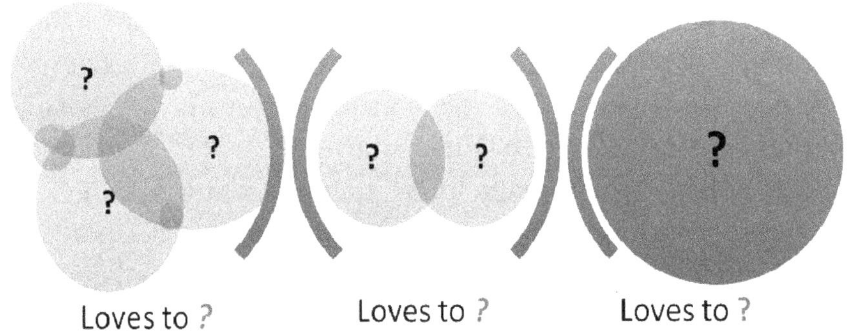

PROSPERITY PLAN:
Prosperity by definition is defined as the state of being prosperous, success, profitability, affluence, flourishing or thriving condition. A prosperous person is therefore someone who is successful (Dictionary.com).

BUSINESS PLAN:
A **business plan** is a formal statement of **business** goals, reasons they are attainable, and **plans** for reaching them. It may also contain background information about the organization or team attempting to reach those goals (Investopedia.com).

WHY DO YOU NEED BOTH?
While I know that it's not common to discuss a prosperity plan, it is vital that it is created outside of your business plan. Your business plan is simply what is says, your company overview and how you envision your business to

be structured, who manages it, how it is being managed, what the products and services are, your competition, who else will be involved, how you plan on marketing the products and services etc. If you are a professional who has made the decision to grow as an intrapreneur within an organization, you can use the same way. On the other hand, your prosperity plan goes beyond your business. It reflects your plan for prosperity in every area of your life: **Physical, Mental/Emotional, Health, Financial, and Relationship**. It essentially looks at every area that can threaten your business plan, if misaligned. Your Prosperity plan starts with your dream goals and slowly moves you into concrete plans on how to make them happen. Just like in your business plan, it provides an exit strategy. The great news about both plans is that they are adaptable and can extend beyond 12 months. Information on how to write a *simple business plan* can be found at the Small Business Administration Official Website:

> https://www.sba.gov/
> https://www.sba.gov/tools/business-plan/1

Want to pick up a **Prosperity Plan Template**? Check out the masterclass: *7 Days to Release Your Amazing Life*. Find out the difference between a business plan and a prosperity plan.

EVERYONE NEEDS A PROSPERITY PLAN. It goes beyond a business plan.

> www.storytellerbistro.com

Never devalue your humble beginnings. They are the seasons of your life which add character to your existence and provides you with the wings to fly high.
DR. PRINCESS FUMI HANCOCK

6. GROW YOUR PASSION

You will only get great at what you focus on. This is your life. Write Your Own Story and Your Own Ending.

Once you turn your passion into profit, it is essential that you have the tools to "grow it." Here, my goal is to present to you the tools you need to authentically grow your business and /or your professional career. It is not enough to finally know what your passion is and how to turn it into profit; you must have the right tools to bring prosperity your way.

Again, many businesses or careers fail if attention is not paid here. How many of us have built a business, gotten people excited about it, then it suddenly fizzles out? Great care must be paid to your business (or career) here if you are to succeed in the long run.

How do you proceed?

(1). You must periodically check yourself. That is, your own skills as the CEO of You Inc. You must identify your areas of weakness and where you thrive the most.

(2). Once you have identified those areas, you must not waste any time trying to do it all. Find people who complement your strengths. Hire them or bring them in as partners. Either way, get the idea that 'you can do it all' out of your head and get down to business!

(3). You are the CEO so begin to act like one, by doing whatever it takes to make what you have turned into profit grow.

(4). As the CEO, you must educate yourself on the various aspects of your business and yes, including the financial, operation, and marketing. Take classes if necessary. Your role is to take your company from *zero to hero, depending on your goal, which is stated in your cash flow (see Day 3- Launch It Phase for your cash flow discussion).*

(5). You must understand the inner workings of your cash flow. Your cash flow report is the backbone of your business. It tells you exactly what you need to be earning monthly and without it your company may be headed for hard times, and you won't even know it.

* It is essential that you revisit your cash flow on a weekly basis; perhaps daily at the on-set. This will help you to push through fears and focus you on what you must accomplish **daily** to make this work for you.

The fact that you have made it to this point proves that you are a winner already. Now it is time to simply duplicate and continually manifest that which you already are, but on a grander scale... so do not allow anything to intimidate you.

When you surround yourself with great minds, you will accomplish greatness. It begins with you as the CEO of your own company or career.

(6). Depending on the type of business or career you are involved in, you should reach out and be part of organizations; first within your own community and then nationally. As you place your business (or yourself) in front of influencers, it will improve your financial bottom-line.

(7). It is amazing what we can accomplish now with the social media platforms. Today, I use Periscope and Blab

TV to showcase what I do. I am currently on Periscope (@1PrincessofSub:
https://www.periscope.tv/1PrincessofSub) where I provide spirituality, mental wellness motivation /inspiration. In addition, provide publishing tips as a publisher.

CAUTION:

Here is my caution where social media is concerned. While they are a great way to get visibility, you must figure out which ones' work for you, then stick with them. Do not end up becoming a social media junkie who is only popular on social media but not meeting your financial target. YOUR GOAL IS TO USE THEM TO CONNECT, BRING AWARENESS and MAKE MONEY.

(8). As you grow, you must constantly assess your skills, products and services. How can you improve upon them to satisfy your consumers? The late Steve Jobs and David Bowie were masters at re-inventing themselves. If you have not read up on them, please take the time to study them. Find out how they re-invented their businesses and kept going. Now, they have a legacy that keeps getting stronger, even with their passing.

Just as we stated in one of our previous lessons, our goal is to leave a legacy behind that generations from now will be proud of. Legacy is what we seek the most and the engine that drives the locomotion, called *YOU*, Inc.

(9). Learn from the best in your field. List at least *3* people who are doing what you are doing and are very successful at it. Then you must learn from them. There are several ways you could learn from them:

(i). By reaching out directly to them and interviewing them;

(ii). If they have books out, purchase them and digest;

(iii). If they are speaking at an event, attend and learn;

(iv). Be willing to invest in your dream! Hire the as your coach!

In conclusion, you may be wondering why this section is short. This is intentional. Simply because this is where you are expected to place your CEO cap on and begin to design what works for your company.

In this section, I have hopefully stirred you enough with success wisdom, to get you start writing a concrete plan suitable for your company.

Having said that, I need you to re-iterate what you have learned from this section:

What is your Take-A-Way?

Develop an Action Plan to Grow YOU, Inc. (The following is a PARTIAL TEMPLATE – **FULL TEMPLATE in MASTERCLASS-**www.storytellerbistro.com).

Make a List of Your Current Products/Services (If applicable):

____

____

____

____

____

____

____

____

____

____

____

____

____

____

____

____

____

____

____

____

____

____

____

____

____

____

____

____

____

____

____

____

____

____

____

____

____

____

Are There Any Plans to Add New Skills, Products/ Services?

TODAY'S DATE: _________

Yes or No: _______________

(If Yes)
0 – 3 months from TODAY'S DATE:
Yes/No___________

Make a list of the new products and/or services:

____

____

____

____

____

____

____

____

____

____

____

____

____

____

____

____

____

____

Your *Expiration Date* for Implementation: ________

Out of these life experiences come character
to sustain our vision.
DR. PRINCESS FUMI HANCOCK

7. SUSTAIN YOUR PASSION

It is one thing to discover or recover your passion, it is another sustain it.

To sustain what you have, it is essential that you adopt daily habits the wealthy and successful cultivate and the poor ignore. If you are one of those who are desperately looking for ways to turn your passion, no matter what it may be, into profit, you do not want to miss this step.

It is one thing to discover, ignite, launch, live, turn into profit and grow that passion but it is most important that what you have grown, you are able to sustain it.

You may have heard the saying, *no man is an island,* while it may sound cliché, it is very true. For you to be able to sustain what you have grown, it is essential that you surround yourself with the right team. No matter how terrific you are as the president of your own company, if you do not recruit the right people with the right gifting, the right motive, tenacity, and commitment; the business may run quite well initially but it will fizzle out. How many times have we heard of a famous business chain who is doing well, only to later hear that they have filed for bankruptcy?

The foundation we build at the onset is therefore pivotal in our overall success. Not only must we be great at what we do, that is, as the CEO, but we must understand that we do not have to be great at everything and that we must learn to allow others who complement us in their skills to do exactly what we have hired them to do.

My Experience?

I remember working for one of the largest healthcare organizations in the US. I was hired into a position, which had never existed in the history of the company. My boss was ecstatic about hiring me because she had done her research and knew the skills I was bringing. I too was incredibly glad as that was not only a great salary package, but I felt the position was going to challenge me and allow my creativity to flourish.

Once I joined the organization, sadly that was not what happened. My boss spent most of her time trying to make sure that no one knew what I did, the other half making sure she held onto those projects she had originally hired me for. After months of frustration, I asked her to come to lunch with me. I point blank asked her why she hired me. She, of course, looked flabbergasted but stated she felt I could be of service in shaping the new department. I asked her what the issue was and why she felt the need to highjack all the work. Her response was that she was used to just doing it all and that she felt it would take time trying to explain the process to me. My response to her was to assure her that my role was to support her, to make her look even greater in the presence of her bosses; to lift the load off her shoulders and not to usurp her authority. She let up for a little while but was soon back in her old ways of doing things especially when her boss started praising me.

Why am I sharing this experience with you? What I soon found out was that she was not settled in her own skin and afraid that someday I might outshine her, and she could be out of a job. This was a sad situation, which yielded nothing productive… just more frustration.

You do not want to be that kind of boss. If you hire someone, you have got to let him or her do their job.

As the CEO of your company, you are charged with ensuring that your company makes money. The more expert hands you have on deck, the better. Ultimately, who you surround yourself with can and will dictate the outcome of your business and even family life.

In my book: Release Your Vision Torch™: *A Blueprint for Success* I discussed 3 major concepts:

Dream Makers, Dream Breakers, Circle of Influence

These three concepts are interconnected. A Dream Maker is one who inspires, motivates, empowers, and challenges the best out of you. A Dream Breaker is quite the opposite, while the circle of influence is the space they both occupy in your life.

As we rise, we must be very careful who occupies our space. Dream Breakers are simply time wasters. While building your business, you simply do not have the time for dream breakers. Dream breakers are simply who they are, if allowed to get close to your dream, they will and can crush your efforts.

For those who have been following me on Periscope, I have taught on several crucial topics: Identity Crisis, Identity Theft, and Vision Crisis.

Here are a few conclusions I stated in some of the scopes:

(1). You are a Fearless Visionary;

(2). That Fearless Visionaries Tear the Veil ™, that is, they are transparent;

(3). That Fearless Visionaries know how to get out of their own way and allow the Creator to accomplish His divine purpose for their lives;

(4). That Fearless Visionaries ™ are "Valley Shakers™";

(5). That the experiences garnered from their valleys qualify them as "Mountain Movers ™";

(6). Being a Mountain Mover ™ pushes them into becoming World Changers and World leaders.

Where Am I Going with This?

Once you understand yourself, it is important that you *watch your circle of influence*. Many of you are experiencing setbacks right now because you are attempting to birth your destinies in front of those who do not belong in your circle of influence, or perhaps those whose time has expired in your circle. Sadly, not everyone will be happy about your promotion; not everyone who says, "congratulations, I am praying for you" are truly happy or praying for you.

Many of you have aborted your dreams to go where you have no business going, and now you may find yourself asking God why things are not moving fast or moving at all. Therefore, it is important that as you progress through this book, taking a hard look at your friends and people who speak into your life is CRUCIAL… that is a MUST, if you are ready to change the course of what is happening in your life and to begin to live the life you are meant to live.

In life, there are **DREAM MAKERS™ and DREAM BREAKERS™.** You must learn to discern the two in your life and know what actions to take when they confront you. If you are unable to discern between the two in your life, then you are headed for trouble.

Dream makers do not just sing your praises, but they are also there to correct you when you are derailed. They help you to focus on the task ahead even when you do not want to hear it because they have your best interest at heart. They do not take no for an answer and so they call you out if need be!

This is discussed in detail: (Circle of Influence is discussed at length). **ORDER Release Your Vision Torch**: Success Blueprint for Achieving Your Dreams, Igniting Your Vision, & Re-engineering Your Life Purpose. As you usher in a new season of re-engineering your Life purpose, you must candidly examine those who surround you and ascertain who they are in this season, in your life. There are many whose season may have ended and yet because of familiarity, you keep placing them where they do not belong. When you do that, you are only setting your clock back. This is where you will need your journal to make this a COMPULSORY assignment… a difficult one to do but NECESSARY if you are ready for success.

Do not forget to **ORDER** your Journal: **365 Days to Release Your Vision Torch *Journal*:** Achieve Your Dreams, Ignite Your Vision, & Re-engineer Your Purpose:
PURCHASE HERE NOW:
Amazon:
http://www.amazon.com/gp/bookseries/B017WCHMHW/
Barnes & Nobles:
http://www.barnesandnoble.com/s/Fumi+Hancock/

In addition, this is when you need to start preparing yourself for monitoring at an advanced level: ***Virtual* and *One-on-One*.** I have said it many times, only a fool thinks they do not need mentorship and if you must pay for it, then put the money aside and invest in yourself. You must know that you are worth the investment!

Several months ago, I wrote an article on my blog: www.yourinneryou.com about DREAM MAKERS™ and

DREAM BREAKERS™. I share that with you now to continue this lesson. This is a very important part of this lesson and PLEASE DO NOT SKIP IT.

Now What?

We are now at crossroads where we get to decide how we want our year to look like. Granted God helps us by prodding us towards his designs for our lives. However, unless we first accept the plan he has for us; then prepare ourselves for it; it will only be a dream.

I am sure many of us have heard the adage: "The grave yard is full of dreams, visions, and goals unfulfilled; novels and Life stories never written, inventions never discovered, music never written, movies not produced…" and the list goes on. It is my sincere desire that none of my Fearless Visionaries will be part of those statistics!

> *To succeed in life, you must*
> *first get into the battle! No one*
> *will fight your battle for you!*
> *So, get in the game now!*

How do you get in the game? By investing in yourself: Time, Money, and whatever it takes!

MONEY

I know! Many, once they hear money they start to shrivel! Truth be told, you are already spending money on things that may not necessarily earn you interest or add value to your future! If we want to be one of those who are successful this year, real financial success, we must never be afraid to hear anyone mention money. So, at some point, like me and every other successful person I know of, you will have to invest in yourself and dream! There is no way around it. If you find someone who is adding value to your life, you owe it to yourself to invest in that value stream!

TIME & EFFORT

We are all very busy people and sadly many are busy circling around the same mountain, not yet willing to do what it takes. Time is a valuable commodity and when we do not have time to invest in ourselves, we might as well pack up and write a big FAILURE sign on our foreheads. If you are too busy to be available for assistance; if you are way too busy and cheap to invest time, effort and money towards your own success; then you are not ready for it.

We make time for what matters the most to us… PERIOD!

As we wrap up this course, let's decide to choose wisely where our dreams are concerned. Fearless Visionaries study, they make unshakable commitments towards their goals, they are not swayed when distractions and make no excuses. More importantly, they do not stop at one exposure to possibilities. They keep going by educating themselves and getting involved.

In conclusion, it is my heart desire that you have already benefitted from this journey called, Release Your Amazing Life, and that you will take it to yet another level by registering for 7 Days to Release Your Amazing Life. There are specialized Virtual, Group Coaching, Success Club, Mastermind, and One-on-One mentoring opportunities for you to explore: *Knowledge is Power.*

8. PAY IT FORWARD

We have the power and the ability to ignite our world for good or evil. It's a matter of choice.

Congratulations, you made it! You persevered and worked to improve your overall success in life. This is what separates truly successful people from those who are not. You were serious, determined, and focused. These are the qualities required to birth an amazing life.

Now that you are here, you are not only ready to impact your own life, the lives of your family members, but more importantly, you want to start living out your legacy. Remember the legacy statement you wrote at the onset, this is what I am referring to here. Legacy is an important part of living and what we do with it matters.

What Then is the Next Step?

This is where we must begin to think about giving back to our communities. What makes the world go around is being able to provide the same opportunity afforded us to someone else. We have the power in our hands to determine what that looks like.

While many may conclude that they want to wait till they become millionaires before reaching out to help others, it is important that we understand that if we are unable to help lift someone up when we are on our way up, we may never do it.

What does help Look Like?

This may look like teaching, coaching, providing resources, or even financial backing for someone else. This may also be reflected in your duplicating yourself. That is, duplicating your passion. Ensuring that you can pass knowledge down to others: *Live Life Full! Leave It Empty!*

Success demands that you also pull someone else out of the hellhole. Now we take inventory on all you have learned, and you will design a concrete plan for you to help someone else. For me, I love my philanthropic work in Africa where I take care of children and sponsor them to school from the grade school level all the way to college level. My non-profit organization, Princess of Suburbia® Foundation (www.adassafoundation.org) has helped set up a state-of-the-art library in my kingdom, Emure Kingdom, in the western region of Africa. As we can raise more funds, we are looking to build Youth Centers in various African communities.

Story Behind My Paying It Forward

What makes the world go around is being able to provide the same opportunity afforded us to someone else? We have the power in our hands to determine how that looks like.

Well over 35 years ago, I emigrated to the United States of America. I stayed away from Africa because I was dealing with a bitter divorce from the man my family initially doubted was my husband. I was filled with guilt, shame, and regrets that my marriage had failed. I felt like the "prodigal daughter" whose parents lost what they had, and I could no longer paddle my way back home. My parents forgave me after finding my children and I struggling… haven lose our home, car, my two-day care centers… all I had I had handed over to a man who could not be counted on. Unchangeable love. When my uncle was coronated as the next king in Emure kingdom, where I originally hail from (in Nigeria, West Africa), it was the perfect time for me to re-unite with my royal roots. In this chapter, I share my own life journey back to Africa… my commitment to mother Africa, starting with the 45 children I take care of in Emure kingdom, under The Princess of Suburbia Foundation, Inc. (The Adassa Adumori Project).

What we do for others will last a lifetime. What are you willing to do to impact the world around you? How are you going to make a difference?

Decide right now; choose what you will do to help others. Do not wait till you have all the financial resources. JUST DO IT!

> *We can't be selfish; we can't*
> *be self-centered, and we can't*
> *be greedy!*
> *Simply Intentional.*

(The Adassa Adumori Project) (http://adassafoundation.org/) .

The following is a partial picture of the 50 children I singlehandedly send to school. In my 10 years of starting this non-profit, we have served over 500 children and we need more support to make this happen for other children. Many recipients of the scholarship have become college graduates and productive persons in the society. More importantly, they are in their communities giving back too.

It is so rewarding to see the legacy building plan this will be to you. Legacy is not only about leaving inheritance for immediate family. It is also about impacting the world at large. Touching lives, saving lives, building others so that they too can create legacies worth sharing with the world. I accomplish that by ensuring quality education and health for youths in Africa.

Regardless of how you may feel about Oprah, she is leaving an incredible legacy of acute business savvy and philanthropy. Though she does not have a biological child of her own, she continues to sow into the lives of young ones in the United States of America and the continent of Africa. Microsoft Bill Gates and his wife run their non-profit organization – educating youths is the core of their non-profit.

Think about this, there is hardly any successful person that do not have a cause they are supporting. Here is my question to you, what are you doing to impact the world today, regardless of your current situation?

See YOU at the Winner's Circle!

Believe in yourself! Have faith in your abilities! Without a humble but reasonable confidence in your own powers you cannot be successful or happy.
Norman Vincent Peale

*You are never too old to set another goal
or to dream a new dream.*
C.S. Lewis

CONCLUSION
YOUR "VISION" INDICATOR

A PERSONAL QUIZ

Character cannot be developed in ease and quiet. Only through experience of trial and suffering can the soul be strengthened, ambition inspired, and success achieved ~ **Helen Keller**

While this is not your traditional school, it is still essential that we gauge where we are with all that we have learned in this journey.

Here are some questions you should ask yourself as you embark on your own success walk. Only a fool will pick up and start a journey without counting the cost. It is important therefore important that you are authentically honest with your answers; take time to really think about each answer that you provide. Remember, this is for your eyes only unless perhaps you choose to show them to an accountability partner who will help to keep you stay focused on your goals.

Strength does not come from winning. Your struggles develop your strengths. When you go through hardships and decide not to surrender, that is strength ~ **Arnold Schwarzenegger**

(1). What does it mean to have an *Inner Genius* and what does it have to do with Success?

Define "Inner Genius" from your own perspective. i.e. What do you understand it to be?

(2). Why would you need to reconnect or ignite your inner genius?

(3). What is the link between finding your inner genius and running a successful business?

(4a). Is life purpose the same as ones' inner genius?

(4b). How can one find ones' life purpose or inner genius?

(5). What are some life keys necessary for igniting your passion or vision?

(6). For those in transition, is it ever too late to live ones' dream?

(7). What are the devastating beliefs or self-talks/lies that we often buy into that stop us from achieving the success we desire?

(8). How do we overcome these devastating beliefs or self-talks?

(9). What role does a concrete Vision Map play in fulfilling your life goals?

(10). Having gone through this experience with me, what major steps must you take to begin on the journey to harnessing your inner genius for optimal success?

MY PASSION MILIEU™

Before I took My Passion Milieu™, I was ready to plunge into a business venture which, with all indications looked right fit for me, until my encounter with this process. Thank heavens that I had taken the initiative to first undergo this program before spending my life savings! As for me, My Passion Milieu™ is priceless. Because of the thought provoking questions, I was spared from spending over $80,000 on a business venture that would have eventually packed up. Do not underestimate what you are getting.
It is a life saver! It is worth every penny I spent, and lots more.
~ Laila O, Attorney at Law, New York City

If you are struggling to uncover who you are so you can lay hold to the works of your hands in an effective manner, then it's time to take a serious stroll through your life. Unpeel the layers, find the trends of your vocation, contrasts all your titles and discover your innovative genius between the grid lines.

My Passion Milieu™ was designed after one of my popular masterclasses: *How to Write Your Passion Plan*. If you are struggling to uncover who you are so you can lay hold to the works of your hands, then it's time to take a serious stroll through your life. Unpeel the layers, find the trends of your vocation, contrasts all your titles, and discover your innovative genius between the grid lines.

My Passion Milieu™ is a matrix packed with practical tools and tricks to help you maneuver through your discovery or uncovering. It helps you to uncover your truths about where you are – if you are on track or you have missed the way a long time ago. It is a necessary juncture checking station where lies, truths, uncertainties are all unveiled.

Get ready to face the giant in your life which has been blocking your path through these years. Get ready to uncover the secret habits which may have hindered you, a while back. Be ready to gain clarity with your message to the world.

> *You are your message to the world. So, what is your message?*

Your legacy cannot be clear until you have discovered your identity. Your identity will not make sense until you uncover your message, and your message to the world are your legs to the world. Your message, once it is validated, grows wings and flies across the globe. Your message brings you influence. Your message and influence unveil, your ultimate brand.

Instructions to find the message behind what you do:

1. **Page 1,** list all the titles you have called yourself and their associated messages. Add each name and related message in the following boxes. Note the date for each title you or someone else gave you.

2. **Page 2:** Think deep and reflect on Page 1 and note when your titles and messages changed. Ask what was going on that made you want to change. What was the trigger that made you call yourself that title or that prompted someone else to call you that?

____

____

____

____

____

____

____

____

____

____

____

____

____

____

____

____

____

____

3. Find your primary message by highlighting those titles and messages that are similar, and then copy them on to Page 2.

4. **Page 3:** Find your secondary message by looking at the messages on Page 1 and circling any titles or messages that are different and copy them on this page, which is Page 3.

Copy your primary messages that you highlighted in the previous pages, here. That is, post them on this Page.

Copy the secondary messages which you circled on Page 1. Post them here for clarity.

Find your innovative ideas

5. Compare your titles and messages on pages 2 and 3 to see where they meet. This juncture is your sweet spot and what makes you unique.

6. With this question in mind, go back and review anything you did not highlight. *"If I knew I would never fail, and money was not an issue, and I wasn't afraid of anything, what would I do?"*

Reflection Time:

1. Did you get any new revelation?

____

____

____

____

____

____

____

____

____

____

____

____

____

____

2. Where and when did your messages collide?

3. What is your primary message?

4. What is your secondary message?

5. What makes you unique?

ACTIVITY: Let's see how focused you are:

As an Advanced Nurse Practitioner, I was trained to care for patient using this: **ADPIE**: *Assessment, Diagnosis, Plan, Implementation and Evaluation.* I have developed a process that is based on this nursing theoretical framework: **VFFEA:** *Valuation, Findings, Forecasting, Execution and Appraisal.*

- Your Candid Thoughts about your revelatory journey
- Have you truly been on course with your plans? If not, why not? (Remember, no excuses)
- Scale your level of faithfulness to the task

Ask a least two people what they think about YOU and what they have observed where you are concerned with your plan. Have you been faithful the journey? (You need people who will tell you the truth)

(i). Valuation
- Your Candid Thoughts about your revelatory journey
- Have you truly been on course with your plans? If not, why not? (Remember, no excuses)

(ii). Findings: How would you diagnose where you are right now? A nurse could diagnose a patient as having fever after looking at the assessment level. Likewise, with Life Mastery, it is important to create some findings.

E.g. If you discovered that you have been making excuses and you keep promising to do something which you never get around to doing, that is **PROCASTINATION**.
Your findings can be positive too. Either way, you need to define and come to some findings. You must examine and know where you are before you can determine where you are going.

____

____

____

____

____

____

____

____

____

____

____

____

____

____

(iii). Forecasting: It's time to do some planning.

Forecast what you will be doing at specific times moving forward. **That is, Design a 30-day plan ~~ Passion Achievement. Plan for 15 Day Check Point.**

DRAW UP A "30-DAY CALENDAR"

(iv). Execution: It is time to put some feet to what you have forecasted.

You have forecasted what you what to do or what you ought to be doing. Here, you are going to map out how you intend to get from A to Z of your forecast. **Do Weekly Plan, breaking it down to daily?**

____

____

____

____

____

____

____

____

____

____

____

____

____

____

____

____

____

____

____

(v). Appraisal: It is time to evaluate what you have accomplished thus far.

15 Day Check Point Observation (Do not proceed any further until you accomplish this)

(1). What Are Your Successes?

(2). What Needs Adjustment? And Why?

(3) Map out your plan to adjust?

30 Days' UP, what have I accomplished and where do I go from here? Evaluate your daily accomplishment & discovery

For example:
Sunday – My Discovery:

____

____

____

____

____

____

____

____

____

____

____

____

____

____

____

____

____

____

Consider expanding this to **60 Days**, **90 days,** which will all flow in the same pattern but build on your 30 days discovery. Create the template again.

Sign up for the **FREE NEWSLETTER**
(http://www.yourinneryou.com/finding-my-dream-makers-
and-my-dream-breakers/)
for wisdom nuggets from Princess Fumi's vault, sent via
email: successlaunchbp@theprincessofsuburbia.com

Like our Facebook Page for updates:
https://www.facebook.com/storytellerbistrofans/

The Vision Empowerment Clinic™ ~ Find out about its
launching by following us on Facebook
https://www.facebook.com/storytellerbistrofans/

Storyteller Bistro Podcast: Free Download
https://www.spreaker.com/show/storyteller-bistro-podcast

RESOURCES: BONUS PACKAGE

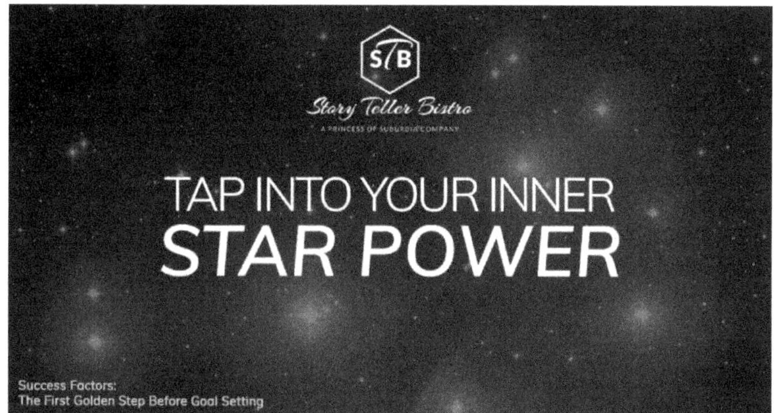

www.storytellerbistro.com
Storyteller Bistro Podcast: Free Download
https://www.spreaker.com/show/storyteller-bistro-
podcast

5 Minutes Success Launch Blueprint
The Series: *Discover, Ignite, & Live Your Passion Fearlessly,*
Without Going Broke!(TM)
https://www.spreaker.com/user/the5minutesuccessblueprint

OTHER BOOKS
2RESPECTMYLIFE SERIES

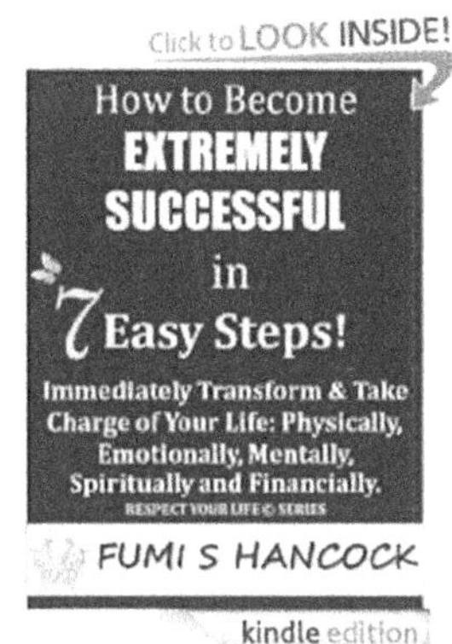

HTTP://WWW.AMAZON.COM/FUMI-HANCOCK/E/B0092OE8QC

OTHER NON- FICTION BOOKS

http://www.amazon.com/Beyond-Worship-Stephanie-Ogunleye-Hancock/dp/1602664765

http://www.amazon.com/Starting-Right-Now-Empowerment-Self-fulfillment/dp/0595205275/

Your Vision Torch™ Series
https://www.amazon.com/Fumi-Hancock/e/B009BHBI6S/

https://www.amazon.com/gp/product/153291007X/

http://bit.ly/ffearless-visionaries-teartheveilbook

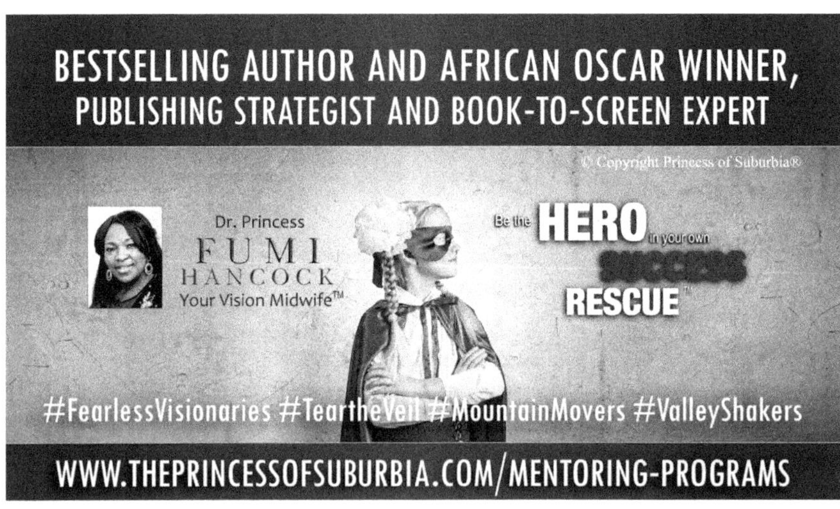

http://bit.ly/millionaireinfluencersecrets

NEW PROJECT
NAFCA African Awards "African Oscar" Winner
Fearless Visionaries Tear the Veil- The Book

ABOUT THE AUTHOR

Dr. Princess Fumi Stephanie Hancock, DNP., M.A., BSN, B.A.

Bestselling Author, NAFCA African Oscar & Indiefest Film Award Winner, TEDx Talk Int'l. Speaker, African Heritage Leadership Recipient, TV Personality, DR. FUMI: The Doctor of Nurse Practice™ Show &Transformation Interventionist, Philanthropist

Dr. Hancock with her love for the literary arts and behavioral health sciences, she has managed to strike a balance between the two, through her TV /Radio shows, documentaries, feature films, books, and her mental health-wellness presentations. To date, she has written over 21 books, 11 of which have become bestsellers and on the heels of releasing other books in the success development, health & wealth arena. Her book series, Your Vision Torch™ has been received by organizations, ministries, and colleges, in Africa, USA, Pakistan and other countries as a success strategy tool. Quit Your Job in 90 Days as equally allowed her to speak in front of Moslem women from all over the world, who converged in London, United Kingdom. In 2018, she got an incredible opportunity to be the first black woman to grace the stage of TEDx Talk-Al Anjal National Schools in Saudi Arabia.

When she is not writing or making movies, she is a sought after International Public Speaker, (a member National Speakers' Bureau & Women's Speakers Bureau-USA), with interesting topics ranging from spirituality, mental health, & wellness, self-help development, personal & success growth. She has been invited to train traditional and political leaders in Africa on Innovative Leadership as well as be a keynote speaker in some African Universities during their convocation ceremonies. Her doctoral dissertation, *using mobile application as an adjunct in treating patients with anorexia nervosa (AN) in communities that regard AN as taboo* earned her invitation to speak at the Sigma Theta Tau International Convention in United States of America.

Some say she is a Social Changer; others say a Transformation Catalyst seeking to extend the hand & heart of social justice, and many, call her a Story weaver who strives to bridge the gap between Africa and America.

Dr. Fumi Stephanie Hancock, DNP, M.A., BSN, an African Princess living in Diaspora is an Advanced Nurse Practitioner turned Screenwriter, President of The Princess of Suburbia® LLC (Cambium Break Pictures), and the host of a nominated NAFCA African Oscar Lifestyle & Health

Talk Show, The Doctor of Nurse Practice Show with Dr. FUMI broadcasted by The Princess in Suburbia®. She was a columnist for over two years at The New American Times, Tennessee where she wrote on "Mental Health & the Media" and has been featured in several newspapers such as the Princeton Packet, The Advertisers' News, Tennessean Tribune. Recently, she launched International Diaspora Network and an Online Virtual Incubator for Professionals in Transition & Emerging Creative Entrepreneur.

Her accolades span from Africa to the US, as the most recent NAFCA African Oscar Peoples' Choice Award Winner~ as Favorite Screenwriter, Indiefest & Accolade Global Films Merit Award Winner, and Depth of Field International Film Festival, Woman of Excellence in Films Award Winner. On the heels of her recently released award-winning movie, Of Sentimental Value, she launched a woman-centric radio show, The Southern Warrior Sister-Tribe which is gaining grounds globally from her homestead, Nashville Tennessee.

Her greatest achievement besides her husband, Dr. David Hancock & their 4 grown children is her philanthropic work in Africa (The Princess of Suburbia Foundation). Dr. Hancock's ultimate mission is to inspire, motivate, empower, and equip others; helping them to value themselves, connect/reconnect with their true calling, and live a well-balanced life. Her desire is to create platforms for others who have not had the opportunity to be heard by telling their stories, one woman at a time. September 2015 alongside a Nobel Prize winner, Dr. Wole Soyinka is being honored by the NAFCA Africa Oscar Film Critic Association in Hollywood, California for their contribution to Literary Arts Globally.

Awards of Distinction:

NAFCA (Nollywood Films Critics Association, Hollywood, CA) NAFCA *African Oscar* Peoples' Choice Favorite Screenwriter

Indiefest Films Merit Awards for *Women in Films*

Accolade Global Films Merit Award: *Women in Films*

African Heritage Award: Contributions in Films, Writing, & philanthropic work in Africa (African Heritage Festival Nashville, TN).

Depth of Field International Film Festival: Merit Award, Screenwriter

Doctor of Nurse Practice (DNP) in Mental Health with Areas of interest: Self-Image, Eating Disorders in silent cultures, Mood Disorders.

2015 Prestigious Honorary Award by NAFCA *African Oscar* Organization, Hollywood, California.

www.drfumihancock.com www.princessinsuburbia.com www.storytellerbistro.com

MORE RESOURCES

Other Books

www.Amazon.com

www.drfumihancock.com

http://www.theprincessofsuburbia.com/

For information on booking Dr. Princess Fumi S. Hancock BSN, MA, DNP to your next event, please log in to:

www.worldoffumihancock.com /
www.theprincessofsuburbia.com

My Blog

www.yourinneryou.com

My Podcast: Storyteller Bistro

https://www.spreaker.com/show/storyteller-bistro-podcast

My Film Production Company

Cambium Break Pictures/ The Princess of Suburbia Films
For details on her upcoming movies, please log on to:
www.cambiumbreakpictures.com
http://ofsentimentalvaluemovies.com

E-Learning Masterclasses

www.storytellerbistro.com

DR. PRINCESS FUMI STEPHANIE HANCOCK, DNP, MA, BSN.

The Princess of Suburbia® Brand
www.theprincessofsuburbia.com
www.drfumihancock.com
*LITERARY ARTS *FILM/TV/RADIO PRODUCTION
*SPEAKER/COACH
(Psychiatric Mental Health-Wellness Expert for the
Entertainment Industry)

&

Find out about
The Princess of Suburbia® Foundation, Inc.
The Adassa Adumori Project

DR. FUMI STEPHANIE HANCOCK, DNP, M.A., BSN, B.A.

Manufactured in Africa….
Assembled in United States of America….
Dispatched to the World.

This is just the Beginning….
One Event Can Change Your Life Forever!
Be the CHAMPION in your own Story.

©Copyright 2018~ THE PRINCESS OF SUBURBIA®

MORE PRAISES FOR PRINCESS FUMI'S BOOKS

Dr. Fumi Hancock is an incredible woman with an incredible passion to see people, women and men alike fulfill their purpose on this earth. She has witnessed first-hand in her own life, and in the lives of friends and family, huge circumstances and challenges that have come to distract and derail them from the plan and purpose that Creator has created them for.

As you read, I believe you will be freed to dream once again. You will gain a heart-felt determination to become all YOU are intended to be and be moved to action to finish your race despite all odds."

~Snr. Pastor Janet Conley – Cottonwood Christian Center, Los Alamitos, California.

Your Vision Torch is just that, like a light down a dimly lit path, a bright, beautiful, and bold wisdom packed life manual for successful and very soon to be successful individuals.

I challenge anyone to read Your Vision Torch from cover to cover and not be inspired! Truly this has impacted me, and I know many others, to achieve your dreams and goals not just for the sake of oneself, but for us all! Thank You Dr. Princess Fumi Hancock, for all the good you pour into others!

~Interior Designer/Stager

"With hopes of healing herself and helping others, Fumi writes these words of inspiration to others"

~Lynn Miller, West Windsor & Plainsboro Newspaper

"Fumi shares the message of hope in the midst of tragedy."
~ **Star Ledger**

"Dr. Fumi is a breath of fresh air to those who cannot see their way out and have lost hope. She is a modern-day Esther understanding her past, recognizing her season and Creator's timing, while embracing her future. She reigns supreme as a communicator, a visionary, a spiritual giant that the world is about to discover, only we knew it all along."
~ **Dr. Phyllis Carter Pole, Author: Temperament – Your Spiritual DNA.**

Spring Hill resident Princess Fumi Hancock has been riding a wave of success since her new book, The Adventures of Jewel Cardwell: Hydra's Nest hit the shelves in September 2012
~**The Advertisers' News- Spring Hill**

Didn't realize you had other episodes. Just got back you're your channel. I am a new fan! ~**LS**

I don't know how to thank you for your activities and your online TV programming. Creator will continue to strengthen your ability, provide more grease to your elbow ~ **OB**

You are so funny princess. You make me laugh so much ~ **RV**

I love your laughter and the way you approach life, Princess ~ **EB**

More grease to your elbow, Princess in Suburbia. I will keep watching ~ **G**L

Just found your video and I loved it. I am off to watch others on your channel ~**JL**

I came across your channel, Princess in Suburbia USA and found the content to be quite engaging and empowering. Thank you for making us laugh ~**YS**

Your show and the Let's Go Innovate Africa group online is quite inspiring. I am happy to be a part of this movement ~ **KC**

CPSIA information can be obtained
at www.ICGtesting.com
Printed in the USA
BVHW041936030621
608739BV00004B/1119